# Therapeutic
# Playwork
# Reader
# one
## 1995-2000

**Perry E**

**Gordon**

# Therapeutic Playwork Reader one
# 1995-2000

© Gordon Sturrock and Perry Else

ISBN – 978-1-904792-26-0

The rights of Gordon Sturrock and Perry Else as the authors of this work has been asserted by them in accordance with the Copyright, Designs and Patents Act 1998.

Published by Common Threads Publications Ltd.

Wessex House

Upper Market Street

Eastleigh

Hampshire

SO50 9FD


**T:** 07000 785215

**E:** info@commonthreads.org.uk

**W:** www.commonthreads.org.uk

Further information on the work of Perry Else and Gordon Sturrock can be found by visiting www.ludemos.co.uk or emailing: info.ludemos@virgin.net

# Contents

# Introduction

This Therapeutic Playwork Reader is the first in what we expect will be a series of papers exploring the therapeutic element of playwork.

The Reader aims to achieve two related functions. Our work has been available from us and from the internet for a number of years; we agreed early on that it was important to get the work 'out there'. Yet increasing numbers of students and playwork professionals have wanted to access the full collection of papers; so here they are. And because of the samizdat nature of our publications – written and published in our spare time between other work – we have had little or no academic review of this work. With this publication we would like to change that and we welcome critical review of these works, with the aim of increasing our understanding of this wonderful thing called play.

In this collection of papers, we show the development of our work up to and beyond the '**The Colorado Paper**'. Written in 1997 for the triennial meeting of the International Play Association, USA, that academic paper was the introduction of psycholudics to a wider audience. The paper reflects our experiences in forming our concepts about psycholudics, the study of the mind and psyche at play.

**The Colorado Paper** states that the play of itself is a therapeutic process for those playing and that play is of fundamental importance to human development and not just diversion from 'more important' activities.

This paper first brought into the public arena the following key terms: play cues, play returns, play frames, ludic ecology, the metalude, play drive or ludido, playwork containment, dysplay, play adulteration, playwork authenticity, playwork interventions.

> '*More than anything else* **The Colorado Paper** *demonstrated that authoritative work regarding the relationship between playwork and the phenomenon of play could be written by and for playworkers without reference or apology to other more established disciplines.*' [1]

The papers we have collected here show how thoughts and models were developed and expanded, then adapted for different audiences. This approach necessarily means that some elements are repeated, yet we have decided to include them all here unrevised. Many of the papers were written 'for their time' and include contemporary references that already seem dated; again these are presented unrevised. We believe each paper has something to offer and the whole compilation is useful for seeing the development of key thoughts.

**Gordon Sturrock and Perry Else**

Ludemos Associates, 2005

---

[1] Mick Conway, Bob Hughes, Gordon Sturrock (March 2004), *A Personal List of Events*, Review of the Values and Assumptions, PlayWales 2004

# The Sacred and the Profane

Gordon Sturrock

## Some Background

This paper is an extract from a larger piece which proposed that playwork – the discipline of those who work with children at play – faces a variety of threats which require it to re-think and re-state its purposes and practice.

I contend that a new paradigm is needed which more effectively describes the essential exchanges of playwork. This new approach, I argue, is a therapeutic model. I see play not as a behaviour, though it could have behavioural outcomes, but as a drive, a ludido. The containment for this ludic instinct within playgrounds, sites and buildings, has some parallels with the analytic frame of psychoanalysis and analytical psychology and with the methods of many therapies, the key difference being that while a number of therapeutic endeavours could be seen to be the archaeology of neurosis, playwork provides a beneficial engagement at the point where such neurosis was being acted, or perhaps more appropriately, played out.

The playworker may use, as is stated of the eminent psychiatrist, Russell Meares:

*'...the field of play to cast a bright light on the developmental ontogeny of the sense of self. He describes in depth the characteristics of the child and caregiver relations by which enduring patterns are laid down that subsequently provide the fateful core of self experience.'* [2]

It is in this tender territory that the playworker is operative, at the very heart of those experiences that the playworker becomes a player, in a web of psychodynamic activity. What a writer says of Meares' ideas is that he sees 'play as the principle metaphor upon which an approach to the evolution of the self is built'. Might it be that our work in play is akin to that of therapy, as Stanislav Grof suggests; in that:

*'Whatever the nature and power of the technique used to activate the unconscious, the basic therapeutic strategy is the same: both the therapist and the client should trust the wisdom of the client's organism more than their own intellectual judgement. If they support the natural unfolding of the process and cooperate with it intelligently – without restrictions dictated by conventional conceptual, emotional, aesthetic, or ethical concerns – the resulting experience will automatically be healing in nature.'* [3]

---

[2] Russell Meares (1993), *The Metaphor of Play*, Aronson Inc. Northvale. N.J., U.S.A

[3] Stanislav Grof (1985), *Beyond the Brain*, University of New York Press USA

4

The irony of the many challenges which playwork faces is that they offer a means through which we may be able to arrive at a more transcendent description of our work and its values. If playwork is to thrive it must learn to authenticate the most fundamental aspects of its practice and draw into its methods elements from a variety of sources. These may help us elucidate the contents of our own practice, its symbolic resonance, as a means of describing a new form of play; one which contains its own healing. A curative potentiality, unlike most therapies, which allows that this healing is constituted not in the power and knowledge of the adult, but in the play of the child. I hope that playwork can come to believe, like Sidoli and Davies, that:

> 'Playing and pretending are like a halfway house between inner and outer reality. This leads on to play and to imagine a playground in the mind and on to the adult capacity to give the inner playing and imagery an outer form in terms of enriched work and living. It could be said that the quality of life depends on how far we are able to play out and live what is within us.' [4]

## Play and Numen

As part of this new vision or re-vision we are obliged to accept that play and the ludic have a numinous dimension. Even if playwork, or the simple engagement with play more generally, is not within the strictest definition of that term therapy, it is at least therapeia; the Greek origins of the word see it as being in service of the gods. Is play a form of devotion to the gods of the playing child and the ludic adult?

We begin with the vision of original play creating life and life creating original play. I use the word 'original' to denote play that is pre-human, pre-cultural, before all conceptualisations and learned responses. Play is a gift of Creation, not an artefact of culture. It is the still point and energy from which all else is evolved. [5]

It may be impossible to define play. It represents an energy which operates outside of all that is known. It can be seen in the gaps in our language – the Freudian notion of parapraxis is very precise – as a monad, after Leibnitz, an irreducible energy like love, with which it has a close affinity. Indeed, in the east, out with the traditions of Western classicism and a Judeo/Christian perspective, play can be understood as *lila*; in essence, play and the ludic, seen as having a religious purpose', or as Mircea Eliade said of dance, an extra-human purpose.

In Sanskrit lila is seen as the cosmic play of the gods, as it is in Hindu mythology. Similarly, in some teachings, connected with the worship of the Lord Krishna, John Lash describes it as:

---

[4] Mara Sidoli and Miranda Davies (1988), *Jungian Child Psychotherapy*. Karnac Books, London

[5] Fred Donaldson (1993), *Playing By Heart*, Health Communications Inc, Deerfield Beach, Florida, USA

*'...a paradigm in religious and metaphysical teachings of the East. In Hinduism, the world is produced from the dreaming of Vishnu, a kind of hide-and-seek game in which the supreme Lord who is dreaming us plays at being us, so that he can delight in the countless ways of discovering himself.'* [6]

David Spangler envisages play as a necessary phase of creative experimentation in the inceptive unfolding of a new spirituality. In Zen, as expounded by Suzuki,

*'...it informs and energises a satori, enlightenment, which stands at the point where potentialities are about to actualise themselves... It is in fact the moment itself, which means that it is life as it lives itself.'* [7]

Hodgkin saw play as akin to the central method of Zen 'to keep alive a creative sense of play'. The yugen of Japanese Noh theatre he sees as an 'emotionally heightened readiness for feelings and ideas.' [8] The Zen master, in a curious correspondence with the Barthes' notion of the photographic punctum is seen as a clown or idiot in an effort to open a new perspective on existence; Enid Welsford's punctum indifferens, or the 'fool as emancipator'.[9] A casual reordering, which Conrad Myers describes as that playfulness which cannot be 'netted' and outlines an ambiguity which itself heralds that 'wondrous playfulness' that moves within all phenomena, disturbing all the labelled drawers of the mind, emptying them and sporting with all their contents, returning both form and content to the inexhaustible source of their being.[10] Heraclitus' 'time is as a child playing draughts' has a particular ludic resonance.

The devotional path Sufism is sought through a process – the Arabic saf, pure – which is unconditional and is arrived at through a kind of selfless ecstasy. There is an aspect of the Sufi Theory of Creation called the Renewing of Creation at each instant, or, at each breath, (Tajdid al-khalq bil'anfas), directly connected with spiritual realisation achieved through a form of playfulness. The dancing of the whirling dervish has overtones of playful behaviour. Henry Corbin, the great commentator and writer on Islamic liturgy wrote, in a form curiously redolent of the mission of psychoanalysis:

*'Ta'wil, is, etymologically and inversely, to cause to return, to lead back, to restore to one's origin and the place where one comes home, consequently to return to the true and original meaning of a text. It is 'to bring something to its origin... Thus he who practices*

---

[6] John Lash (1990), *The Seekers Handbook* , Harmony Books, New York, USA

[7] Dr T Suzuki (1977), *Living in Zen*, Rider & Co., London

[8] R.A. Hodgkin (1985), *Playing and Exploring*, Education Paperbacks, Methuen & Co., London.

[9] M. Conrad Hyers (1974), *Zen and the Comic Spirit*, Rider & Co., London.

[10] M. Conrad Hyers (1974), as cited

*ta'wil is the one who turns his speech from the external (esoteric) form [zahir] towards inner reality [haqiqat].'* [11]

The great Sufi poet, Rumi, captures the tawil – the transfiguration of a literal event into an image of soul, as the Sufis would have it – when he writes;

> *'Last night the moon came dropping its clothes*
> *in the street.*
> *I took it as a sign to start singing.*
> *Falling into the great bowl of the sky.*
> *The bowl breaks. Everywhere is falling everywhere*
> *Nothing else to do.*
>
> *Here's the new rule: Break the wineglass,*
> *and fall toward the glassblower's breath.'* [12]

Or in a more direct fashion:

> *'Out beyond the idea of right doing and wrong doing there is a field. I'll meet you there.'* [13]

In Tantrism, the serpent of kundalini is an energy that impels the devotee towards liberation. A liberation, of which Mukerjee writes:

> *'... is considered in Indian life to be the highest experience – a fusion of the individual with the universal. The individual manifestation is like a spark of the cosmos, as the human organism, the microcosm, parallels everything in the macrocosm.'* [14]

Ramakrishna describes the kundalini consciousness as follows;

> *'The very distinction between 'I' and 'thou' vanishes: Whenever I try to describe what kinds of visions I experience when it goes beyond this place ... and think what kinds of visions I am witnessing, the mind rushes immediately up, and speaking becomes impossible. In the final centre, 'the distinction between the subject of consciousness and the object of consciousness is destroyed. It is a state wherein self-identity and the field of consciousness are blended in one indissoluble whole.'* [15]

A view not far removed from modern ideas of quantum physics, Fritjof Capra, in his 'Tao of physics' discusses a 'Hindu view of nature' in which all forms are relative, fluid; an ever-changing maya conjured up by the great magician of the divine play. On Taoism he is moved to quote

---

[11] Henry Corbin (1988), *Avicenna and the Visionary Recital*, Bollingen Foundation, Princeton University Press, Princeton, N.J., USA

[12] Noel Cobb (1992), *Archetypal Imagination*, Lindisfarne Press, Hudson, N.Y., USA

[13] Fred Donaldson (1993), *Playing by Heart*, Healthcommunications Inc. Deerfield Beach, Florida, USA

[14] Ajit Mookerje (1989), *Kundalini*, Thames and Hudson, London

[15] Ajit Mookerje (1989), as cited

Chuang Tzu, as an example of the polar opposites which dynamically operate in a continuum of flux:

*'The 'this' is also that'. The 'that' is also this. That the 'that' and the 'this' cease to be opposites is the very essence of Tao. Only this essence, an axis as it were, is the centre of the circle responding to the endless change.'* [16]

Schiller, the German Romantic idealist, saw the 'play-impulse' as essential for the human personality to balance and reconcile the opposing thrusts of material and spiritual concerns. He suggested that:

*'the essence of all aesthetic experience lay for this earnest mind in the activity of play (Spiel)'. He countered the essential negativeness of Kant's definition of aesthetic experience as 'pleasure without any practical interest' and turned it into a positive ludic dynamism: 'Human beings only play when they are in the full sense of the word human; and they are only fully human when they play.'* [17]

Within the mythic firmament a kind of playfulness can readily be seen within the ludic perspectives projected by such figures as Pu tai, Loki, Coyote, the holy fool of Zen and Hermes. It might be useful to spend some time in examining this latter personification, Hermes, the psychopomp, the guide of souls. Kerenyi sees this, as:

*'The sum total of pathways as Hermes' playground; the accidental 'falling into your lap' as the material; its transformation through finding – thieving – the Hermetic event – into an Hermetic work of art, which is always something of a tricky optical illusion, into wealth, love, poetry, and every sort of evasion from the restrictions and confinement imposed by laws, circumstances, destinies – how could these be merely psychic realities? They are the world, and they are one world, namely that world which Hermes opens to us.'* [18]

We can see a continuation of this thought in Nietzsche's ideas on the contrast and connection:

*'Between the Apollonian (the serene sense of proportion which Wickelmann had so admired and which found its crowning expression in Greek sculpture) and the Dionysian, (that flood which breaks through all restraints in the Dionysian festivals and which finds artistic expression in music). In Nietzsche's later works the Dionysian no longer signifies the flood of passion, but passion controlled as opposed to passion extirpated, the latter being associated with Christianity.'* [19]

---

[16] Fritjof Capra (1921), *The Tao of Physics*, Flamingo, London

[17] T.J. Reed (1991), *Schiller* Oxford, University Press, Oxford, England

[18] Karl Kerenyi (1992), *Hermes, Guide of Souls*, Spring Publications, Dallas, Texas

[19] Walter Kaufmann, Ed. (1976), *Portable Nietzsche*, Penguin Books, London

## The Constellation of Hermes

Within this cosmology we can see, projected in the figure of the Greek god Hermes, the suspended Lila function. The ludic potentiality has become constellated within the depth psychology's appropriation of mythology to its own practices. Hermes, and the hermetic function, is thus neuroticised. Jung wrote that 'what were gods are now diseases'. Is the neuroticising of neurosis necessary to the maintenance of the seriousness of therapies and analysis? From their playful first contacts, Freud saw free association as the fundamental rule of analysis. Can we trace a denial of the ludic in their extensive narratives?

The Hermes connection continues to appear, symbolically, as a kind of alterity, a hologrammic potentiality. An implicit order which contains within it, when looked at from a numinous standpoint, the idea that every divine form comprehends itself within the essence of all things. This may serve to illustrate the logical fertility of the stance that play and the ludic has some form of religio/magical status and standing. In short, that mythically, it can empower and carry the will to encounter between a microcosm and a macrocosm.

Einstein mapped an alternative route when he said that all science begins in 'myth'. He went on to say that:

> 'The psychical entities which seem to serve as elements in thought are certain signs and more or less clear images which can be 'voluntarily' reproduced and combined... This combinatory play seems to be the essential feature in productive thought – before there is any connection with logical construction in words or other kinds of signs which can be communicated to others. The above-mentioned elements are, in my case, of visual and some muscular type. Conventional words or other signs have to be sought for laboriously only in a secondary state, when the mentioned associative play is sufficiently established and can be reproduced at will.' [20]

Jung, as one might expect, appeared to show a certain devotion to imagination and to playing: (the prefiguring action of all creativity)

> 'The creation of something new is not accomplished by the intellect, but by the play-instinct acting from inner necessity. The creative mind plays with 'the object it loves'... we know that every good idea and all creative work are the offspring of the imagination, and have their source in what one is pleased to call infantile fantasy. Not the artist alone, but every creative individual whatsoever owes all that is greatest in life to fantasy. The dynamic principle of fantasy is play, a characteristic of the child.' [21]

---

[20] Steven Pinker (1994), *The Language Instinct*, Allen Lane, Penguin Books, London

[21] Jung as quoted by James Hillman (1992), *The Myth of Analysis*, Perennial Books, New York, USA

Hitherto, this drive, out of the ideas of Freud and Jung, has always been appreciated from solely within the depth/psychoanalytic perspective. Their mythic conflation means that it is laden with either Oedipal or hero/senex metaphoric currency. But it can now be seen as being something more simple; namely as playing.

Hillman advises that we may be required to rethink psychological work.

> *'If soul-making is not treatment, not therapy, not even a process of self-realisation but is essentially an imaginative activity of the imaginal realm as it plays through all of life everywhere, and which does not need an analyst or an analysis, then the professional is confronted with reflecting upon himself and his work.'*

## Play and Therapeia

We might, in play, be able to offer a contribution to this rethinking of the therapeutic practice. A new paradigm might emerge from the basis of two new approaches, or tenets, for our work in play. These are that the process that this view outlines, the flow 'as it plays through', is really what I describe as the ludido. Elaborations within the psychoanalytic context seemingly use the hidden and cryptic play motif to describe solely the sexual content of this questing desire. Adam Phillips writes of the need to 'outplot' the Oedipal, the ways we get round our Oedipus complex is our Oedipus complex.' [22] Perhaps this desire to outplay, or to outplot, is a sign of a ludic *juissance*, or as I have previously written, is it rather a 'jouer essence'?

The second tenet is that we are required to function within a space of healing potential; an encounter which insists that we reflect deeply on the task and its symbolism. As T.S. Eliot shows:

> *'And he is not likely to know what is to be done unless he lives in what is not merely the present, but the present moment of the past, unless he is conscious, not of what is dead, but what is already living.'* [23]

The signal failing of playwork, and indeed, of our understanding of play more generally, may be that we refuse to recognise that it has a potential, not simply in the material manifestations which so preoccupy us, but in a delicate, precious and sacred psychic ecology. An ecology of affect which the child encounters with an open heart and one which we see fit to deny as a measure of profane adulthood.

Huizinga propounds a further statement with which to approach a definition of play, one that sees it not as a behaviour, but as a drive, or instinct operative in this sacred hinterland.

---

[22] James Hillman (1992), as cited

[23] T.S. Eliot as quoted by Thomas Ogden (1994), *The Subjects of Analysis*, Karnac Books, London

The spirit of playful competition is like a social impulse, older than culture itself, and pervades all life like a veritable ferment. Ritual grew up in sacred play; poetry was born in play and nourished on play; music and dancing were pure play. Wisdom and philosophy found expression in words and form derived from religious contests. The rules of warfare, the conventions of noble living, were built on play patterns. We have to conclude, therefore, that civilisation in its earliest phases played. It does not come from play like a baby detaching itself from the womb; it arises in and as play and never leaves it.

**Gordon Sturrock**

November 1995

# A Diet of Worms

Gordon Sturrock

*'The aspect of things that are most important for us are hidden because of their simplicity and familiarity.'*

Ludwig Wittgenstein

## The Setting

Playlink ran a series of seminars in 1996 led by Bob Hughes, entitled 'Addressing the Fundamentals', which covered a range of linked topics. The titles were, first, 'What is play? Why make provision? Second, 'What is playwork, what is it for?' The last was, 'What makes a good play environment, and why?' During the group discussion on 'What is playwork?' a key issue emerged that I would like more fully to explore. In my view, the essence of the discussion will help, as it helped me, to understand what is unique to playwork and how we might begin to articulate the reflective element of our practice.

It might be useful to outline the essential structure and process of those seminars. They were well attended with over 30 participants. Those who took part ranged across all the various types of provision and from part-time, face-to-face staff, through to managers, researchers and even the odd academic. By and large, the grouping could be characterised as being experienced and committed. The sessions began with a paper from Bob Hughes to us, ensemble. This was then amplified through the smaller, group sessions; the resulting discussed material was fed back to the larger group. The smaller groups were facilitated by a key person in each of the smaller units; the final plenary session was usually led by Bob himself. The material generated was written up and distributed to the participants. Bob's initiating papers were also made available.

I would like to concentrate on the exchanges of one of the small group discussions. It must be said that the resulting outcomes led, in no little part, from the very able facilitation of Stephen Rennie, from Leeds Metropolitan University. (It is not my purpose to submit a verbatim or comprehensive report of the detail of the group dynamic and interchanges. This is a personal and annotated explication. It is not anything other than my own individual and impressionistic, hindsighted account.) It is an attempt to develop two key themes which emerged from the encounter, namely;

- Playwork and the judgement calls playworkers are obliged to make
- What might constitute the reflective nature of playwork

After his initial paper, Bob Hughes posed the question, 'What did we *feel* about playwork?' I have added the italics to give emphasis and highlight that aspect that our group chose to work on; principally, the emotional or affective elements of our practice and, as a consequence of this, what we accordingly felt about playwork.

Once this approach was accepted, and engaged with, it became immediately clear that this presented members of the group with a difficulty. We, who have been occupied with the practice of play, have very little opportunity to discuss precisely that range of exchange we share with children, as it impacts on us as emotions, as feelings, or (to borrow a term from the therapies) as affect. This dimension is largely considered to be extra-mural to our playwork task. Yet it was obvious, from the very tense nature of the opening discussion that this was a topic area and approach, which was eliciting a certain and discernable response. Even if this reaction, in the first instance, was one of unease, nervous tension, fidgeting and avoidance of eye contact. Matters which, in the parlance of the depth psychologies, could be construed as resistance, defined as: 'the name... given to everything in the words and actions... that obstruct(s) gaining access to (the) unconscious'.[24]

There appeared to be a distinct evasion of the affective content, perhaps of the contact with unconscious material generated by the question, evident through the use of verbal constructs such as, 'I think,' rather than 'I feel', by those group members who did speak. Others chose to remain silent. The first point that can usefully be made is, when examining the affective elements of our practice, we have very few prescribed means for this exploration to occur. We have a limited affective/emotional vocabulary to describe our work. We are forced to travel in an inscape for which we are professionally, and perhaps, personally untrained.

Note I do not say that we do not have feelings about our work. I am suggesting that we have no established mechanisms or methodologies to 'fix' these emotions and feelings into the frame, the matrix of meaning, of what is coming to be known as 'reflective practice'. Yet it is, in my view, out of this element of our work that we essay the judgements that we make on a minute-by-minute basis in the course of our working days. This forms the essential theme of this paper.

## The Provocation

During the course of the group exchange, Stephen Rennie prompted us with a series of case questions. These served, not just to illustrate the various and sometimes peculiar incidents which underpin our work, but to show the kind of continuum of judgement within which playworkers are required to operate. As a sub-theme it also provides evidence for a core description of our work; namely, that of 'judgement workers' in the child's play environment and experience. These are points I will attempt to return to throughout this piece. However, to address the question that set this response into motion, I have to indicate again that I am interrogating my own thoughts and evaluation, alongside my impressions and interpretations of those of my companions.

---

[24] Laplanche and Pontalis (1973), *The Language of Psychoanalysis*, Karnac Books, London

Stephen Rennie set the following poser: 'A child on your playground is chopping up a worm. What do you do about it?'

I'll let that question sit in a paragraph of its own for a moment. For me, it arouses a certain return to experiences of my own; I can for myself recollect similar incidents occasioned both out of my own playwork and out of my own childhood. One of the purposes of worms may be, I somewhat unsympathetically offer, precisely to function as the stuff of this protoscientific quest. It is neatly mirrored in the beginnings of biological science where the worm is dissected as part of the school curriculum. Whatever the background, we playworkers are confronted with our fictitious child and the equally fictive worm. The responses from the group were interesting. I categorise them, crudely, here:

- Some would intervene because there were agreed rules on the playground; for example, those which respected the rights of all living things. (This latter explanation could also be seen as a post-intervention rationalisation.)

- Others would intervene and had strategies for so doing. Amongst these was a form of intervention that explored the shared feelings between the child and the playworker. I would describe this as the 'Have you any idea how horrible that makes me feel' approach. (The child invited to enter into an affective/emotional space with the playworker as a means of measuring and evaluating their behaviour.)

- Several thought that the chopping of one worm was not a cause for concern but if it became, say, eighteen, then this might trigger a response suggesting that there was a degree of compulsive or pathological intent to be met with. (Eighteen is an arbitrary figure and merely outlines the observance/intervention cycle that playworkers are obliged to work within.)

It is not for me to suggest that any one of these categories is 'correct' or that one judgement should somehow prevail over another. I will suggest that this judgement formation, implementation and contemplation, should and can be set into forms that permit us fully to explore the implications and to develop our idea of reflective playwork.


## Explication

Igvar Johannson, talks of kinds of patterns that I have adapted and out of which, I hold, it may be useful to examine our responses to the child at play. He states:

*'All behaviour is performed and learned in specific environments in relationship to specific behaviour-contingent events what is learned is not a behaviour pattern but a* **behaviour-environment-event** *pattern.'* (my emphasis) [25]

---

[25] Igvar Johansson, as quoted in Kent Palmer (1995), *The Social Construction of Emergent Worlds* (manuscript)

If as playworkers we encounter certain behaviours and cues – the sometimes subtle and not so subtle cues and invitations that the child fires off to the environment, other children and adults who are within that particular frame – we can couch them within this contextual outline, though I will make one crucial addition to the concept. To begin.

We may see the child playing in a form that is, of itself, contained and self sustaining; that is the child fully engrossed and caught up in the act of playing, the fantasy, with whatever object or artefact pertains. No cues are being fired off that require the involvement/intervention of the playworker, or indeed, other children in the actions. (I ought to interject that what I say here can also be true of a group of children; I use the individual child only as an explanatory form.) The specific play drive is being satisfactorily met and is bounded in a self-contained feedback loop. The role of the playworker in this situation may be solely to sustain the external environment so as not to impede the play; the so-called 'gate keeping' function.

Huizinga writes of play, that:

*'It is a significant function – which it is to say, there is some sense to it. In play there is something 'at play' which transcends the immediate needs of life and imparts meaning to action.'* [26]

If we are to respect this idea we may be required to absent ourselves from this most 'immediate frame' of the play. He assumed, '...that play must serve something which is not play, that is, it must have some biological purpose.' [27] Therein lies an irony, in that we may have to admit that when we work with the playing child, we sometimes serve that which is 'not play'. This 'not play' may well define with some precision a key role and functional dimension of playwork and the playworker. Essentially, to be aware of a prefiguring aspect of play, which is latent and perhaps symbolically represented – *as it appears to the child but solely to the child or group of children at that time* – acknowledging it by a *judgement* of active non-participation. I, the adult, am abiding in *not*-play.

The playworker's actions are to preserve the space within which this form of play is being enacted but not to be directly involved, the play is not guided and the playworker is therefore in the 'not-play' state. The Greek idea of the *temenos*, as a sacred enclosure, has some resonance for this notion. The playworker preserves the sanctity of what Winnicott describes as the 'potential space'. All of which might, in terms of our original worm question, be represented by a judgement suggesting that no intervention was necessary. I would describe this play enactment as a fully contained *behaviour-environment-event* cycle. The emphasis, for us, is however on the behaviour-environment aspect of the formulation.

---

[26] Huizinga, as quoted by Russell Meares (1993), *The Metaphor of Play*, Jason Aronson, Northvale, NJ, USA

[27] Huizinga, as quoted by Russell Meares (1993), as cited

The next level is where the playworker is serving not this 'not play' but is, or becomes, directly involved in the child's playing, having followed up a specific play cue. In terms of our worm criteria this might include such an invited intervention as engaging the child in the 'how that makes me feel' response. There are of course any number of others that might be used; I will not enumerate them here. What I will offer is that this intervention broadens the pattern we have discussed into a *behaviour-environment-event* pattern or cycle.

The playworker has, by the very nature of their involvement deepened the child-held, contained cycle, into an event. I say deepened not to suggest that the child's initial experience was not a profound one, it may well have been, but that the worker then concluded that it fell into the 'not play' category. Now, however, the very involvement includes *the child's play and a playwork-based contact and exchange*. The child's ludic drive and its objects and artefacts, the environment, now encompass an additional potentiality; namely, the playworker active in the dynamics.

It is this dynamic, seen as the *behaviour-environment-event* trope, which forms the essential nuts and bolts of the judgement and reflective element of our practice. In short, the exchange has now become an event, it has heightened or extended potentiality. The most crucial part of our playwork description begins to be engaged and active. This event pattern is an occurrence that may take place any number of times during the course of the work of those in play. It is the remark or resource, the reframing, the arbitration, the adjudication, the reworking of a momentary rule, what generally comprises the commonplace quotidian of our work. Our actions – Foucault usefully describes this power as 'action on the actions of others' – can be reflected upon against the background of our aforementioned pattern. That having been understood, I would now like to broaden the range of category or qualification, introducing what might be termed a transcendent aspect to the proceedings.

When we begin to evaluate our response within this arrangement we also add a dimension that Johansson did not articulate. James Hillman, the analytical psychologist, talks of that, 'unknown component which makes meaning possible, turns events into experiences'.[28] I would advocate that when we reflectively respond to the child, entering the event patterning I outline, we have another layer or level of consideration that we bring to bear. That is, the field of experience from which we trawl our responses; of our own childhood; our play experiences – those which were met as well as those which were thwarted; our play experiences as playworkers in a variety of settings and with many groups and individuals at play; the many post-work sessions where we discuss the events and incidents of the day and everything that could be seen to be part of our ongoing training,

---

[28] James Hillman (1977), *Re-visioning Psychology*, Perennial Library, Harper Row, New York, USA

education and professional development. By such engagement we can choose to deepen the event of intervention into a potentiality of experience.

The behaviour-environment-event pattern now has an additional component, that of experience. The experience of the child at that point in time is now in direct encounter with the experience of a non-typical, non-authoritarian adult in a delicate overlapping but psychic ecology. This I suggest can be understood as the *behaviour-environment-event-experience* pattern.

## The Ludic Ecology: a Topography

The child in encounter with the adult. The perspective is of the child's play drive, the ludido, viewed as part of the reflective continuum of the worker/psycholudic analyst.

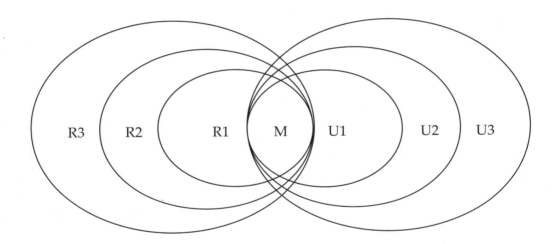

## M – The Metalude Mandorla

The key child/playworker interface. Locus of the child/playwork/er 'event/experience' overlap (after Johansson/Sturrock.) Symbolic of the intersection between heaven and earth (Cirlot). 'Ecstasy of variety'. An internal imaginal zone. Direct linking with the unconscious. 'As-if' potential. No morality. 'Desires' vivification in contained reality. Playful. Free association. Ogden's 'analytic third'. The autistic-contiguent. Winnicott's 'potential space'. Adi Da's 'the bright'. Prefigures all creativity.

| R1 – Contained Reality | U1 – Personal Reflective Potential of Adult |
|---|---|
| Locus of the playwork/child 'event' (after Johansson). The depth psychological/therapeutic process. Creative. Emergent rules, rites, rituals. Expression. 'Desires' incorporation. Vaginal, context, myth and mythopoeia. Animate, Cooperation. Authority by joining in constructed reality. Meaning seeking symbolic affirmation. Bonding. Communication. Mediates æffect.* Image. Eros. 'Paranoid/Schizoid' position (Klein). | Total psychic contents and constructs of the playworker/analyst as potential. Identity and cultural background. Intervention 'event' (after Johansson) in delimited psychic space. Locus of more objective personal experience. 'Desires' æffective congruence and incorporation. Creative. The working 'process'. Anima (female archetypal qualia: after Jung). Transference. Individual reflective component. |
| **R2 – Constructed Reality** | **U2 – Collective Reflective Potential of Adult** |
| Environment (after Johansson). The depth psychological/therapeutic frame. Destructive. Law, found by banishing or artificially imposing containment. Games, including 'sprechte' (after Wittgenstein) 'games of knowledge', rules, ritual. 'Desires' expression. Phallic, text, grand narrative, masterplot. Dominance. Mastery. Symbolic, requires meaning. Morality. Utterance. Logic. 'Depressed' position (Klein). | Total mental contents/constructs of the playworker/s/analyst/s as potential. Environment (after Johansson). Images and symbols in universal form as themes and archetypal motifs. Reductive. Reactions based on understanding own 'desire' for æffective outlet and consequent mediation. The working frame. Animus (male archetypal qualia: after Jung.) Counter-transference. Group/team reflective component. |
| **R3 – Unknowable Reality** | **U3 – Unknowable Unconscious** |
| The Ludido – the child's play drive or instinct which functions through an interplay with surrounding 'fields' to circulate through the metalude, (M): contained reality, (R1): and constructed reality, (R2): seeking, desiring animation, authority and law, text and context, æffective outlet, expression as a means of homeostasis. Circulating holistic, ecology of the conscious and the unconscious. Thus the inner cycling of ludic energy precisely mirrors that of the external environment/world – the ludic microcosm is the same as the external macrocosm – as a form of consciousness. | * Aeffect – Combination of emotion as used in psychology and the idea of effect an outcome or aftermath. So, æffect is emotion or feelings and their outcome or expression seen as a whole. |

It is from this reflective field that we draw those aspects that underpin our judgement. It is also this crucial formulation, which shows how difficult and limiting it is to develop stated and specific protocols of response, to the playing child. We make an elementary mistake when we assume that because the child is not yet mature their capacity to evolve judgement, *only some, a minor part of which will be formed through contact with our capacity, as playworker, to make judgement*, is somehow more primitive or unformed: they are simply more fluid. The child lives in a plethora of choice and judgement, a kind of ludic ecstasy, which they explore in order to form and construct their own lifeworld. It is we adults who live in an enscribed world of job descriptions, non-negotiated social responsibility, power and politics. Erikson writes:

> *'There is a grim determination of adults to 'play roles' – that is, to impersonate to the point of no return their places in a cast forced upon them by what they consider inescapable reality.'* [29]

It could therefore be argued that it is, more tellingly, the adult in the child's play who is the primitive and the child the sophisticate. Erikson goes on to say:

> *'The play construction, then, can be seen as inventively negotiating between the small builder's inner universe and his society's changing world view.'* [30]

The worm question serves well in allowing us to examine this crossover from the event, a child cutting a worm on the playground, to the *experience* of the child cutting one or several worms on the playground with us as the attendant mediators. (The number is merely the most superficial of measures, what we are really, tacitly, discussing is *intent*.) I offer that this intent and action can be viewed in terms of the child's developing inner universe, and resulting world view, and could be read as having powerful and resonant symbolism. Out of world myth there is a useful and applicable metaphoric explication, which could be ventured about our imaginal child cutting up his/her worm, and forms the pivotal point of the event-experience compact. By this amplification we make our responses fit into more sophisticated schema that the child may be unconsciously communicating. If I might elaborate.

## Mythological Content

The great worm, the *uroborus* (there are various spellings, I will stick with this) is a mythic image that has universal functionality. It can be seen in religious traditions, practices and rites across the world. It is a universal motif. It was as relevant for the Aztecs as it is today for the aboriginal peoples of Australia. Erich Neumann, sees it as being a description of a level of consciousness, he says:

---

[29] Erik Erikson (1978), *Toys and Reasons*, Marion Boyars, London

[30] Erik Erikson (1978), as cited

*'The uroborus is properly called the 'tail-eater' and the symbol of the alimentary canal dominates this whole stage (of human development).'* [31]

Wilber advances this by suggesting that:

*'The infant's self no longer is the material chaos, for he is beginning to come to recognise something outside himself, something other than his self, and this global, undifferentiated, prepersonal environ we call the uroboric other.'* [32]

Out of Neumann's work on the history of consciousness, Wilber argues that:

*'The uroboric self already possesses some sort of self-boundary – it is already begging to break the old oceanic state[33] into two global terms, namely the uroboric self versus some sort of 'uroboric other' or 'uroboric environ'.* [34]

Now, it may seem to be far-fetched connection to be making between our worm-enraptured child at play, and these ancient and widely-held ideas and their esoteric exegesis, but is it really that distant? I will argue that it is not, and further, that such knowledge can help playwork begin to explicate the field of judgement and reflection within which we work and where we might place our professional, diagnostic constructions. (When I say diagnostic, I use it in the sense of being relative to our intervention and not as a lapse into a medical model.)

Could it be that our child is in fact arranging their world so that the expression of this inner need, the recognition of internalised states of consciousness, is being externally expressed and must be met? That such material can, in effect, be played out? That the chopping of the worm is, as Wilber outlines, the exploration or celebration of his/her 'self-boundary', the 'break' from the former oceanic state? Is it the recognition of the 'uroboric other' that the child is enacting?

It was certainly recognised as such in more 'primitive' societies. The Australian aborigines couched this cognitively in 'the great snake', the circumcision rites, of their tribal lore. In short, that the sometimes difficult passage of this level or strata of human development were eased by its recognition in the established rites and rituals of the community. Joseph Campbell writes of the role and purpose of myth and the mythologem, the mythic structure, when he says:

---

[31] Erich Neumann (1989), *The Origins and History of Consciousness*, Karnac Books, London

[32] Ken Wilber (1989), *The Atman Project*, Quest books, Wheaton. Ill. USA

[33] The oceanic state is the state of the new born infant, which Wilber describes as when the self and 'the other' are undifferentiated. The change to the uroboric state occurs when the child is forming an opinion about what is 'out there'.

[34] Ken Wilber (1989), as cited

*'Traditional mythologies serve, normally, four functions, the first of which might be described as the reconciliation of consciousness with the preconditions of its own existence.'* [35]

A description, which I suggest, is not all that far removed from the work of a playground. Our *play leading* (to use a defunct term) may be as a kind of guide to the transition of these states, a function accorded to the playful figure of Hermes in Greek mythology.

Tradition, rite, ritual, and myth serve to bridge the gap between that which constitutes our individual view of the world, our collective memory and recall, and reality. A confluence I see as being the purpose of play, literally as an expression of emergent forms of consciousness. Roose-Evans cites Van Gennep, when he says that;

*'He has named this the liminal state, drawing on the Latin word limen, meaning threshold. The initiate crosses over the threshold from one stage to another, and once he has crossed he can never return.'* [36]

He goes on to explain:

*'The significance of ritual is that it constellates a profound experience; it provides a traditionally sanctified opportunity to accomplish a transformation of the ego's experience of the Self... Now I am a boy belonging to my mother – Now I am a boy leaving my mother – Now I am a boy leaving my mother and submitting myself to the ritual that the gods have decreed – Now I die as a boy and am ritually dismembered – Now I am born as a man among men.'* [37]

Playgrounds and playworkers may be positioned to provide this psychodrama, which children need, to carry and contain their internalised but emerging expression. For, where the *rita* are removed by adult conceptions of the world, they are played out in the group cultures of children, in cults, cliques, gangs, societies, trends and tribes. Vandalism, graffiti, extremities of fashion, and so on, are not the child's act of sabotage against the adult world but the re-ordering of the schema we adults impose so that they retain some meaning and identity for them. I cannot but help in seeing clear correspondence between the play of the child at its most obvious level, what we might describe as play at its most manifest level, and those deeper aspects to which I give a certain reading here. This I would describe as play at the latent level. It is perhaps because we live in de-ritualised societies, where there has been the steady erosion of rites of passage for our children, the denial of the latent, that we encounter so much *dysplay*.

---

[35] Joseph Campbell, ed. (1988), *Myths, Dreams and Religion*, Spring Publications, Texas, USA

[36] James Roose-Evans (1994), *Passages of the Soul*, Ritual Today, Element Books, London

[37] James Roose-Evans (1994), as cited

## The Application of Judgement

A child is cutting up a worm on our playground. We as playworkers are asked the question; 'do we intervene?' Our examination of this problem is difficult as it requires us to enter into a field, a morphology of experience, which, within the present descriptions of our work, has no means of explication. It simply has not been articulated, partially accounting for our group's generalised difficulty in bringing these feelings into the light of day. However, these are matters, in my view, which we must begin to grapple with if we are to make sense of the work being undertaken in playwork practice. The judgements that we are required to make, and which may have a signal and powerful effect on the child's developmental processes, are not recorded in what is held as the literature of play. Yet they exist very powerfully in the rich seam of anecdotal material, playworkers almost routinely produce, when they are not concentrating on what constitutes the formal codes of response that plague our definition of the work.

It is legitimate that I can analytically interpret a situation, where our child and that ubiquitous worm may be representing through symbolic form, matters, images and aspects of their emerging consciousness. An understanding of this material readily adds to my ability as a playworker making judgements about the play intervention and content of the child's play. This approach may also have a significant import on the organisation of the environments within which we work with the children. It may, for example, permit us to evolve a more meaningful context for descriptions of equal opportunity than the necessary but limited protocols we have up till now developed. True equality of opportunity, certainly within the play context, lies in the fullest possible exploration of the child's developing consciousness through the various symbolic and mythic forms it may give utterance to or create. The Hindu or Muslim child may well be playing out symbolic, and other material, which has in their own cultures been met by rights and rituals they are denied in what up till now has been a rigidly secular, but politically correct, play practice.

It is perfectly acceptable to suggest that the child on the playground is an actor in an imaginal theatre of their own construction. Their passage through some of this *ludic material* will on occasion require a series of interventions and judgements by the playworker. If the child is in a cycle of play where the playworker sees the pattern I have previously described being repeated, where there may be the first signs of obsessive retentative play, it may be that a sympathetic ritual or rite can be enacted that will allow this passage to be safely negotiated. That this enactment can draw on knowledge of myth, ethnography and anthropology, and some of the analytic, interpretive material, so abundantly available in the depth psychologies, seems to me to be route worth exploring. A field of knowledge with definitive data, which impacts directly on that liminal area, out of which we essay our judgement calls. Judgements, I reiterate, that we are required to make in a context and continuum more onerous than almost any other profession and that may have a profound contributory effect on the child's development.

Such an approach also allows me to set my work with the child or the group of children into an ontological, that is a process related to being, framework.

I can only venture some ideas and guesses about what the being of a child is or may be experiencing. I can be somewhat more assured about what is *going on in me* while these observations, and my resulting mediations and interventions, the *personal context* out of which these determinations, are being generated. It is this and other such material that informs and guides the various arbitrations in the play context I may be required to make. My trust is that the child, not a primitive, but functioning in sophisticated ranges of choice and opportunity, responds to the judgement I demonstrate because it is honestly arrived at, not because it shows a conformity or coherence in the greater scheme of things. I believe that the child's response to my mediation is not something that they take as a given, that is the role of more significant, authoritative others, but that the child accepts and can understand the *honesty of process* through which I arrived at whatever outcome I serve up. They intuit that I am endeavouring to be authentic. This dynamic of understanding effectively forms the event-experience paradigm.

## In Conclusion

I have attempted to deepen the event of Stephen Rennie's question into an interrogative experience. Of necessity this has been out of my own repertoires and ranges of knowledge. It may not either please or appeal to others across the board. What I hope it will achieve, is that when we speak of reflective play and the judgements we make – that we do so through the most careful observation and exploration of what the play form and cue that the child is engaged upon, and its context or setting – means to us both. This understanding is, by its very nature, constructed out of our own lifeworld and its constituent elements. It is held, not by 'me' on behalf of the child, but is the result of an honest and rigorous cross-examination of 'myself' in *relationship* to the child.

I submit that this examination, which I have briefly suggested may be symbolic, mythic and fabulous, is fundamentally *transpersonal*. It is, obviously, open to other and various explorative schema. Whatever the sources, our understanding may be polysemic, carrying a variety of meanings. It is likely that in any number of cases, the reading of one playworker will vary from that of another. Perhaps, the real lesson inherent in the question of our child and the worm is that we must, as a profession, be free to make these various judgements. The key lies in how we account for them to each other, and above all to the children we work with, rather than enshrine them in procedures and responses of rote.

Our new job description might read, as Robert Cushman says:

'*In the extremity of man's plight, Plato offers a defined therapeia. It includes … metastrophe or 'conversion' of the entire soul, involving the affections, by which nous, the organ of cognition, is reoriented rightly with respect to prime reality.*

*Given these terms, Plato's conception of philosophy is such that it seeks the birth of a new consciousness. The clue of course is the Socratic understanding of the philosopher as mid-wife. The Socratic maieutic (from the Greek word for mid-wife) sought only to assist the inquirer in bringing to the light of conscious, rational awareness, the knowledge which was his original heritage, but which has been 'forgotten'. Thus part of the Socratic Method is the doctrine of re-collection or remembrance whereby 'learning' is to be understood not as the transmission from teacher to student of new information. It is to be understood rather as the conversion of the soul, by means of philosophical midwifery, whereby the original knowledge comes once again to light and the seeker is once again oriented rightly with regard to prime reality.*' [38]

**Gordon Sturrock**
February 1996

---

[38] Joseph Campbell, ed. (1988), as cited

# SPICE – a Redundant Metaphor: Towards a More Extensive Definition

Gordon Sturrock

*'One does not discover new lands without consenting to lose sight of the shore for a very long time.'*

Andre Gide

This brief paper addresses the central idea of the '**SPICE**' rationale as it is employed and taught in the measurement and evaluation of play space, play environments and the play experience. I will suggest that the idea that underpins the SPICE notion and the inherent approach it endorses has had its day. That our understanding of play has moved on and that we now stand in a contemplation of factors that it does not include (I use a word with a ludic root advisedly) requiring us to disinvest in certain ideas, which had hitherto held some authority for us.

There is a general acceptance within the play field, playleaders, the play profession, if such a thing exists, and what might be described as the play literate, that the use of the SPICE trope – or misuse that the author implies accompanies the acronym – provides a quantitative tool for the value or worth of the play experience; the so-called 'play value' conundrum. It is my intent to show that we must look at more sophisticated means to examine the essential interplay at the heart of the play exchange and its values. In short, that a new metaphoric currency should form our operational model of measurement of play and the ludic. (I should make it clear that this paper is an initial attempt schematically to present what will, I hope, be a more fully explicated matrix of meaning for play to follow.)

It might be useful to remind ourselves that the SPICE acronym is deemed to essay:

**S** Social

**P** Physical

**I** Intellectual

**C** Creative

**E** Emotional

as the contents of the play experience. Accordingly, any analysis of play value is contingent on our reading as being reductive to one or several of these categories. These elements therefore are thought to constitute the basic, some might say, essential ingredients of the play encounter and the world. It offers, presumably, an opportunity to measure, to produce a taxonomy of the play experience. Indeed, it has come to stand for and to be represented as just such a means. I believe that in actuality it imposes a synthetic and solely manifest description on play.

The principle problem in the SPICE method is that it has no place for the viewer in the frame. It presents only a part prescription in that it assumes that I, the observer, the applier of the technique, am somehow out of the picture. SPICE is worked by an externalised non-participant effector. The meaning of an exchange or an artefact is consigned to be other than its actual experiencing. It proposes an objective fallacy. The child at play or an environment that can offer, can contain some of the highly internalised fantasy construct of their imaginal play, stands to have some or all of it disregarded as it falls outside of the SPICE equation. And, if the method we employ permits only partial and inaccurate measurement of play environments and experiences, dealing steadfastly, and only, with the externally obvious and manifest content of the ludic qualia, then it should be reconsidered in this light.

SPICE cannot tackle the core of the issue, the coming to terms with the deeply internal and symbolic, the idea of meaning in play and how we approach it. As Erik Erikson puts it:

> 'We thus learn to grasp the fragility of that 'I' with which we learn to begin so many utterances as we speak from a central 'point of view' (a Gesichtespunkt as the Germans would call it) attesting to views more inclusive than the sum of facts we can be sure of, and appealing for a communal actuality, which must help our orientation.' [39]

SPICE does not allow the fragility of this point of view, namely the seen or felt subjective. It presents as having a knowledge base but offers only information. It allows no commerce between the internalised hopes, fears, aspirations and ideas of the child at play and the function of the environment as a container to hold this projected content. Neither does it expose the vulnerability of the evaluator/expert who appears to be surveying the method. The child's drive to play and the projected cues and responses they draw from that environment, are eliminated from the 'objectivity' of the paradigm as offered. There is no scope for the numinous, for the inclusion of the spirit of play, where the worth of play maybe in *projected* play content, or as a space where identity and our understanding of the self is generated.

To be blunt, if SPICE should reflect back to us, mirror the essence of play, its values and meaning, are we happy with what it portrays?

Is there not a better way for us to examine the content of the play experience and the potentials of space both physical and psychic? Can we not develop a formula that is less reductive and more inclusive, accommodating not just hard artefactual evidence and behavioural outcome, but which also examines its expression, as Winnicott would have it 'the creative apperception that makes the individual feel that life is worth living', that is to say, its meaning?

---

[39] Erik Erikson (1978), *Toys and Reasons,* Marion Boyars, London

26

Perhaps we can revivify and evolve the SPICE idea – just as happened when the PIES of nursing and planning was extended – to absorb some of the less tangible and abstract aspects of the ludic: its affects, transferences, its numen and its spirit. Thus we can acknowledge that these are the phenomena that have drawn us to play, as players ourselves, and as a concomitant ingredient of the mix.

SPICE is a filter through which to apply some categorisation of the ludic environment and of play exchanges. However, what we are confronted with, should we choose to measure it, is not simply the environment as a fixed static entity, but rather interactions between players and where and what they play, which has me (I) as an active participant, in what Palmer so tellingly describes as an 'ecstasy of variety.' In my view, we should be assessing the interplays of this ludic ecology, in an inclusive methodology, as a heuristic ideal, rather than that of a viewpoint artificially poised in some 'objective' space.

The question remains: can we develop a more holistic and inclusive method by which to begin to evaluate what play and the ludic? I believe we can. If I might explain.

I propose that the idea of SPICE should be greatly extended and radically overhauled. The problem with any acronym, however well intentioned, is that it becomes a protocol or procedure. By its usage we actually set limits on observation. It has, through familiarity, become merely a substitute for engagement with matters that are abstract and subtle. It is more correctly defined by what it excludes. I suggest that we use a more flexible and pliant form. This new formulation I call **'PISCES'**.

PISCES contains a germ of meaning from astronomy and astrology. It allows us, just as the constellations have done in times out of mind, to hold a projected idea as a container of meaning. PISCES invokes the female principle of the sign of two fishes that swim in opposite directions emblematic of the creative/destructive cycle of play itself. It conveys the sense of a beginning in the deeper regions of the personal in fantasy and imagination, and a movement to mastery, through layers of play interactions. It contains a thesis of an ecology of play: namely, of a play drive operative in a ludic landscape, an *inscape* as Hopkins so poetically invokes it, as a reflective cycle of projected cue and return.

This confabulation can symbolize the creation and destruction of the ludic as it comes to outward expression. In myth, the symbol of the fish is connected to 'penetrative power' and has 'psychic being' and is held to be sacred. It has been found among the Phoenicians, the Assyrians, the Babylonians and the Chinese. The Chaldiac peoples used it to portray cyclic regeneration. It is associated with 'profound life and the welling up of the life force.' [40]

---

[40] JE Ciriot (1990), *A Dictionary of Symbols*, Routeledge, London

PISCES is not a definitive and self-contained formula. It is rather a matrix, which attempts to delineate both physical and the more internalised psychic content of play, its 'inner psychic reality,' to use Jung's time worn phrase. I have no wish for it to be seen as complete, it must be added to and amended if it to have any worth. It has no author and no authority unless the reader/user becomes part of the picture. But, as a start, I suggest that it might include some of the following in its usage and to which many and much more should and could be added. (If I might reiterate; the point of the PISCES construct is that it is to be amplified, that each idea should be deepened through its application within the personal dimension that the user brings, and it is to be added to. If the PISCES idea, through usage should become redundant and be replaced by some self-generated dictum, so much the better.)

Nevertheless:

**P** – Play in general, but we must also consider that which is Personal to us and to the Playing child; our Participation in the Process; that some of the content of that which we observe will be Physical but that there is also the Psychic to be evaluated; and that we should always be aware of our Perspective and how that is formed/being formed and its impact on our evaluation/involvement.

**I** – We must understand that our Identity is formed in a community and particularly among what are described as caregivers; Intelligence, both ours, and that of the child, in conjunction and collusion with the Intelligence of site. We are required, as Grof indicates, to 'cooperate intelligently with' the environment and the play ecology.

**S** – The greater part of play, not least in its internalised mode, is Symbolic. We might also include the Spiritual. Outside of our Western perspective play is understood as having a sacro-religious aspect. Also that this is the field within which our idea of the Self is generated. As it is said of the eminent psychiatrist Russell Meares, he: uses the field of play to cast a bright light on the developmental ontogeny of the sense of self.

It could also contain the idea of the *Socius*, as proposed by Deleuze and Guattari, as being 'the community which holds our identity.'

**C** – Out of play is generated all Creativity. It is also about our Considerative Craft within play. But, perhaps most importantly, it is the Culture within which the child, the playworkers and the site have to live and work and wider Culture more generally. What is/are the predominant Culture/s? What are its values, its artefacts and archetypes, to which we should give attention? It is also our Contemplation and reflection on our play and our involvement in the play of others. Finally, it is about Celebration, the sometimes individual and sometime universal, celebratory rites and rituals that we enact on the playground or at play more generally.

**E** – The play Ecology, the generalised aspect of the child's play in the Environment that obtains, as an aspect of well-being, of health; the Events of the playground and their potential to be changed, through meaningful contact, into Experiences, as Hillman optimistically suggests. The formula, that, after Johansson's useful *'behaviour-environment- event'* paradigm, can be deepened to include Experience. Thus we might be evaluating *behaviour-environment-event-experience* occurrences.

**S** – One element should stand alone: that is Security. But this can be amplified to suggest that security of their right to play: the safety of the site and the people who work there; of our practice and its operative concerns.

The PISCES idea attempts to convey the belief that play is a drive that seeks expression and containment. A reflection, which is both a mirroring back and a deeply considered reflective work method. To do this, we must transparently be part of the play process and not at some remove from it. If we are to measure play it will always be ineffectual, unless we attempt to deal with that great immeasurable: its underling *latent* content and, of course, where we stand in that unexplored, fluid dynamic. Only out of this first consideration can we begin to evaluate the hard physical elements of playgrounds, play sites, toys and so on, as they stand as containers of meaning. A stone may be seen as merely a stone, but to a child at some level of deep imaginal play, it may be blessed with magic and meaning, which we are obliged to record and register in our cogitations.

The pressure on the play environment, and less tangibly the ludic ecology, is no less real than that of other endangered species and habitats. If we can begin to represent the ludic in all of its complexity, we may be better able to counter this threat. The adoption of the PISCES paradigm, where authority rests not in an acronym but in the application of a self-regulated approach and process, promises a more holistically tuned tool for such evangelism.

> *'We are like a stray line of a poem, which never feels that it rhymes with another line and must find it, or miss its own fulfilment. This quest of the unattained is the great impulse in man that brings forth all his best creations.'*
>
> Rabindranath Tagore

**Gordon Sturrock**
February 1997

# Play is Peace

Gordon Sturrock

*'A person's growth, from infancy to adulthood, is simply a miniature version of cosmic evolution. Or, we might say, psychological growth or development in humans is simply a microcosmic reflection of universal growth on the whole, and has the same goal: the unfolding of ever higher-order unities and integrations.'* [41]

## Introduction

This paper argues – by the removal of the settings and sites where our children have played; by the steady erosion of the values and methods that recognised this need and enabled this playing; by the resulting de-ritualising of the habitat; by the adulteration of the ludic process; by the imposition of adult agendas and programmes; by our failure to recognise the power and purpose of play – that we contribute to the breakdown of an essential homeostasis, of what is, in effect, a ludic eco-system and ecology. The drive to play accordingly seeks expression (which it must) in ways, in signs and symbols that are aberrant, deviant or disturbed.

Our young are creating lifeworlds where isolation, violence, predation and predatory behaviour, disruptive and self-damaging acts, are coming to predominate. I argue that this behaviour, I term it *dysplay, is* a compensatory response. To explain: Erik Erikson, remarked that:

*'The play construction, then, can be seen to be inventively negotiating between the small builder's universe and his society's changing world view.'* [42]

My interpretation is that, by any reading of contemporary accounts, our 'small builder's universe' – one that mirrors and reflects our own – shows distinct signs of *dis-ease.* This distress is ours as humankind. It is in this denial, of the play construction in its widest sense, that ensures we are not at peace.

The burden and responsibility in addressing this discord should lie with us as adults, who create it, rather than they who suffer it. I suggest that there can be no idea of peace, as an abstracted, conceptual goal, unless we first address what is the purpose of play in our human development. In fact, I go further; play and peace are the same thing. And unless we come to terms with that, we will remain, as George Steiner, has it, 'monads haunted by communion'.

---

[41] Ken Wilber (1989), *The Atman Project,* Quest Books, Wheaton, USA

[42] Erik Erikson (1978), *Toys and Reasons,* Marion Boyars, London

The task we face requires us to explore what play means to us as adults, all the acts of communication and trials of encounter, and will entail creativity of an advanced order. Hillman sets out the stall:

> 'There is no use taking up any of the usual positions today. We are all so sick and have been so long on the edge of mass suicide and are groping so for personal solutions to vast collective problems, that today, if ever, anything goes. The fences are down: medicine is no longer the preserve of the physician, death for the aged, and theology for the ordained.' [43]

## Play Presently

In Britain, some years ago, there was a brutal murder of a toddler. The perpetrators were two older children. Led by the tabloid press, the nation recoiled in horror. The scene of the van thought to hold the two young alleged killers, being attacked by an enraged throng venting their anger, is difficult to erase from the memory. This mob would have killed had the police not been present *en masse*. The Prime Minister, John Major (not noted for his commentaries on childhood) summed up the situation, saying: 'We must understand less and condemn more'. Yet another scene is enacted that contributes to the covert removal of the child from the environment. It is the enshrining of such ignorance that this paper attempts to counter.

John Major, issues a mandarin dictat that further banishes the child from our understanding to the excluded margins of humanity, as the reprehended shunned. The politician, ever interested in power and the populist nullity, reminds us that the child's actions can be acted against, and so effectively he underwrites adulteration. The victim and those who commit the crime, all children, are the guilty. The innocence is somehow ours, the concerned adult.

In Victorian times, childhood was abrogated by labour, images of dark mills and climbing boys. Presently, similar dominion is fuelled by a projected angst of social fear. This 'midnight of anxiety' is promulgated as a deliberate act ensuring that children are earlier and earlier constrained by adult 'order' and adult 'mores'. We can thus justify conscripting our children into education, mollified by the predicate 'early years' tag, and out-of-school 'playcare' – rapidly becoming a similar confection – as a response to this neuroticised, external environment. As a consequence, it is now not unusual to see children at the age of five spending ten hours of their day in some adult ordained and institutionalised context. Children's play, and the playcare or nursery setting, are coming to replace the mill or factory as symbols of adult hegemony.

Were such a situation to be relevant to some small, cuddly animal – say, a cross between a hedgehog and a hamster – activists would be

---

[43] James Hillman (1989), *A Blue Fire*, Perennial Library, Harper Row, New York, USA

scouring the country setting up reserves. They would establish hospitals with 'widdlytinky' names and would picket the despoilers of the grounds where our 'hoghams' live and prosper. Television personalities would be campaigning and fronting programmes where the lifestyles of our favoured creatures would have their most intimate habits exposed in the name of their preservation. Soon, hoghams – now thoroughly anthropomorphised (the cartoon/puppet show was a big success, the toy an all-time best seller) – are once more abroad on the commons.

Perhaps, what we see happening with children is the beginning of this formation. They now stand as some kind of alienated 'other', a necessary exclusion and a prior process to their re-induction into grown-up culture as a bastardised acceptability. The task of providers of pre-school education and playcare is increasingly in this kind of membership consideration.

The result is that the ludic habitat is thoroughly adulterated. Nowadays it must be recognised that when we provide a play environment, a statutory obligation under UK law, we do so as a substitute provision. Those charged with the work of free play – a field in which we were at one time world leaders – now do so within forms of containment that are artificial. And, if the argument is that playgrounds are unnatural (compensatory might be a more fitting term), then it follows that we must ascertain that the stuff that goes on within them, our day-to-day, adult, involvement, is as child centred and sensitised as we can manage. We are required to acknowledge that we function within a recreated space, which mirrors a deeper and more profound, naturally occurring pastoral, of the child at play in the environment.

It is this recreated environment and the consequences of our attitude to it that forms the major trust of this paper. While we seek to educate our children, instil values and ideas that we think sanitize our own futures (and our sins in the past and present) in this compact, the child is little more than a cipher carrying our projected intentions. We overlook the child as a person. Iona Opie, reminds us of this sovereign sensibility, when she writes of the child's view of themselves, not principally as children, but as 'people'. In an emerging discourse on the child (the demesne of fields that privilege the attitudes of adults in what is little more than a licence to practice a developmental jurisprudence), an alternative view offered by the playwork field and the child – the real play experts – is ignored.

A compensation of the worth of play and its contribution to identity and self is given no mature contemplation. Perhaps we must come to see, like Sidoli and Davies, that:

> *'Playing and pretending are like a halfway house between inner and outer reality. This leads on to play and to imagine a playground in the mind and on to the adult capacity to give the inner playing and imagery an outer form in terms of enriched work and living. It could*

*be said that the quality of life depends on how far we are able to play out and live what is within us.'* [44]

That is, seeing playing and pretending as entirely natural ingredients of lives, which are not so much peaceful, but based in peace.

### An idea of play: an idea of peace

*'What we are discovering and feeling is original play, the heart-beat of the universe. The question is not whether nations are prepared to find an alternative for contest, but whether you and I, as individuals, have the wisdom to formulate a newly evolved process based on new assumptions and are prepared to live it.'* [45]

In the UK, there is an emerging idea of play that is worth some explication. It is at present in its earliest inception, a 'frontier' area that the existentialist philosopher, Merleau Ponty, described as 'wild being', and is, at least from this writer's understanding, being substantiated in terms that have a religious or numinous dimension. It can be seen in the confluence of physics and religious tradition and in the generalised discourse that attends depth psychology (the founding work of Freud and Jung and their interpreters), and in the therapies. However, little is advanced on these disciplines' dependency on the ludic for healing outcome. From a perspective formed out of a long-time engagement with the child at play, I feel their curative speculations somehow miss the beat. Though beyond the scope of this paper fully to examine this miscellany of misconstruction, a few general points can be drawn.

Einstein said that 'all science begins in myth'. In accord with this dictum I offer the following as a kind of alternative *myth* of play:

Play is a drive or instinct. This has been observed by, among others, Meares, directly, and indirectly by Jung and Freud and their followers. It is mesmerisingly well documented in religious writings of the East. It was also my own observation, which is not important, but this came out of my reflection on my experiences of play as a playworker, which is important. It is a universal mammalian characteristic, and as Huizinga outlines, serves some biological purpose. In recognition of the work of other drive-figured enterprises (such as psychoanalysis and analytical psychology, in particular, and the therapies, more generally), I called this play drive the ludido. This drive can be seen in the subtle and not so subtle cues that the child 'fires off' to the environment and what is in it, artefact or archetype, prop or person. [Attention Deficit Disorder – ADD, the hyperactive tag – in my view is the firing off of these ludic cues, which not being met and returned, are reissued with anxiety in a cyclic display.]

---

[44] Mara Sidoli and Miranda Davies (1988), *Jungian Child Psychotherapy*, Karnac Books, London

[45] Fred Donaldson (1993), *Playing By Heart* Health Communications Inc. Deerfield Beach. Florida, USA

The ludido can be discerned in a deeply internalised form of fantasy play, which I again observed from my play practice, and have confirmed out of my work in the therapies. This internalised zone is variously described, most notably by Winnicott, who called it the 'third area' and the 'potential space'. He invested it with qualities from his psychoanalytic perspective.

To differentiate and to recognise the aforementioned spiritual/religious functions, I describe it as a distinct, operative zone. This I termed the metalude; literally a higher form of play. I suggest it is the locus of the homeostatic balancing between the child and the environment that pertains; a kind of internalised and ludic 'Gaia' process. By 'reading' this balancing process, adult players can contribute to the child's development in a way that is child-centred and integral to their future well-being. This totality I perceive as being a ludic ecology.

The encounter of the child and the adult in any play exchange involves, in part, an overlapping of these zones – the child's and the adult players – to form a new intersubjective identity. Acknowledging Thomas Ogden, I perceive of this conjoining, as a ludic third. This is an interplay that is wholly natural in the child-to-child interchange. Those who are at the cutting edge of analytic practice see this zone as being the locus of their healing. A healing that therapeutic practitioners maintain is constituted in their own interpretive practice, Freudian Kleinian or whatever. I hold that it is the effect of playing, particularly the act of joining in the ludic third, which has the healing inherent in it. (This can also be the case with a group, where there would be a collective overlapping, the point being that the coalescing act is the same.)

When in the course of our enjoyment with the child we enter the zone, effectively the emergent unconscious, the encounter is laden with information that is symbolic and constellated in various collective themes, images and constructs. These Erich Neumann called stadial (stage) developments. He went on to say that their general significance was that:

*'This interdependence of collective and individual has two psychic concomitants. On the one hand, the early history of the collective is determined by inner primordial images whose projections appear outside as powerful factors – gods, spirits, or demons – which become objects of worship. On the other hand, man's collective symbolisms also appear in the individual, and the psychic development or misdevelopment, of each individual is governed by the same primordial images which determine man's collective history.'* [46]

---

[46] Erich Neumann (1989), *The Origins and History of Consciousness* Marshfield Library, Karnac Books, London

The consequence of all this, is that the play encounter, the drive active in the stage, frame, play setting, playground, the toy, artefact, game, ritual, rite, is contained and reflects or is reflected back, to the child or player. This containment 'holds' the meaning or intentionality of the child's play. These 'imaginal loops' are comprised of the symbolic forms of 'stadial' development the child is expressing, and require our acknowledgement with and for them. It can be seen in the various *rita*, established or created, that sustain the enactments they undertake as part of their maturation. When this 'recognition' fails, when the containment breaks or ruptures, or is not fully expressed, we get forms of *dysplay* emerging. The therapies see this as neurosis.

If, almost all psychologies of depth, or therapies, are the *archaeology* of such neurosis formed in childhood, we might, through this kind of engagement, be placed to enable the 'playing out' of possible neurotic formation. This constitutes the core of a new idea of a play-based therapeutic practice where the healing is initiated, not by the adult practitioner, but by the child. I maintain this is an ecological function.

I am not sure whether there can be an attitude (is beatitude a more appropriate term?) which is peaceful. We cannot *become* peaceful without first *being* at peace. Emile Fackenheim, suggests that even: 'As decent and sober a thinker as Immanuel Kant could still seriously believe that war served the purposes of Providence'. History shows that peaceful outcomes are arrived at by subduing peoples and populations. Francis Fukuyama, in his otherwise prescient book on the 'end of history', indexes no mention of peace. The idea of solace or peace would appear to be the purview, solely of religion or philosophy. But, the hope must remain that it can exist in the new synthesis of ideas and an emerging notion of partnership and cooperation: the purpose of play. Fritjof Capra sums it up thus:

> 'These....are some of the basic principles of ecology – interdependence, recycling, partnership, flexibility, diversity, and as a consequence of all of those, sustainability. As our century comes to a close and we go towards the beginning of a new millennium, the survival of humanity will depend on our ecological literacy, on our ability to understand these principles of ecology and live accordingly.' [47]

That these are worthwhile aspirations is beyond doubt. Part (perhaps the most crucial element of our 'ecological literacy') rests in our most internalised and intimate recognition of just this thrust in the play of our children and our own play as adults. Erik Erikson notes:

> 'We thus learn to grasp the fragility of that 'I' with which we learn to begin so many utterances as we speak from a central 'point of view' (a Gesichtespunkt as the Germans would call it) attesting to

---

[47] Fritjof Capra (1996), *The Web of Life* Harper Collins, London

*views more inclusive than the sum of facts we can be sure of, and appealing for a communal actuality which must help our orientation.'* [48]

It may be legitimate to see our environmental *Gesichtespunkt,* formed in the play frame and an essential component of the ludic ecology, as the kernel of peaceful development.

## The New Rule

*'Here's the new rule. Break the wineglass and fall toward the glassblower's breath.'*

Rumi

If, as an adult, I contemplate the idea of peace, I become caught up in its massive irreducibility. It is too large a notion to deal with. My perception can only be captured in fragments, in the moods and sometimes madnesses, that attend the search. George Steiner writes:

*'Even as it forgets or represses the formative drives of childhood, so the immense majority of mankind will experience the solicitations of literature and the arts only very rarely. Or, they will answer to such solicitations only in their most ephemeral, narcotic guise.'* [49]

Could this 'narcotic guise' be a kind of sleep, a movement from an awareness which we once had, but have now rejected out of a profane idea of adulthood? Abjured to put aside the things of childhood, we throw away that which is central to the very heart of our humanity. The banishment from the Garden of Eden was not from an externalised horticultural Arcadia, but an internalised ludic landscape; virtually, consciousness in its earliest state, one that is widely observed and recorded. Piaget thought of it as a 'protoplasmic' or 'symbolic', Ferenczi as one of 'unconditional omnipotence'. The language exploring this inscape, often uses the term 'paradise', or 'paradisal', noting the condition of the neonate and the child as 'oceanic' or 'pleromatic'. Whatever, the primal force of this stratum is propagated in themes that are eternal. Eliade explains:

*'The myth of the primordial paradise, evoked by Plato, discernible in Indian beliefs, was known to the Hebrews (for example, Messianic illud tempus in Isaiah 11: 6-8; 65: 25) as well as to the Iranian (Denkart, VII, 9, 3-5) and Greco-Latin traditions. Moreover, it fits perfectly into the archaic (and probably universal) conception of the primordial illud tempus.'* [50]

What if, as I have suggested that this state is a ludic centre, the idea of a metalude pertains, and is there as an 'always prior' element to all that we encounter, prefiguring creativity, and all other conditional forms or

---

[48] Erik Erikson (1978), *as cited*

[49] George Steiner (1991), *Real Presences* Faber & Faber, London

[50] Mercia Eliade (1974), *The Myth of the Eternal Return,* Bollinger Series, Princeton, USA

appearances? And, rather than being a function we leave behind in childhood, it is an ever present reality? As we grow, we fall – that might be rendered Fall – into illusory self-consciousness. Maturation requires that we conform to the norms of societies, less and less attuned to the need for play, for fantasy, for the imaginal. We perceive play as being a realm only for the child and in so doing we diminish our ludic and creative potentiality. This fall therefore is *out* of awareness, *out* of play, into more primitive, deluded, material currencies.

A delicious irony becomes apparent: it is the child that lives in a sophisticated milieu of potentiality and the adult inhabits one made increasingly more primitive by 'as-if' reduction. We become habituated to a denial of the 'force of fantasy', where this denial has, as a consequence, symptoms of breakdown, of dis-ease, of ecological crisis, as central to our impious, 'adult', egoic demeanour. Is it too large a step to take to say that our idea of the Self is constructed in this emergent metaludic space? Jung's conceptual definition is most useful:

> *'The self is not only the centre', Jung writes, 'but also the whole circumference which embraces both conscious and unconscious: it is the centre of this totality, just as the ego is the centre of the conscious mind'.* [51]

Meares might agree:

> *'For the adult, the inner life of images, ideas, and memories, moves in the mind's eye against a space we know is not real space. It is virtual space. It is as if inner experience is projected upon a metaphoric screen. For the young child, the arena upon which thought is displayed, in toys, is real. In only a partly figurative way we can say that the play space is the precursor of inner space in adult life. It is where experiences are generated that become the core of what we mean by personal selves.'* [52]

The point I make is this: that if this construction of the inner play space, and whatever virtual semblance it takes in the adult is disrupted, the formations that occur will be both disturbed and disturbing. The adult – as much as the child – who has not developed a mature capacity to enter into this state, this *speilraum* – 'playroom' as Freud had it – is dysfunctional and demonstrates dysplay. And in dysplay there can be no solace, no peace. Children often carry this projected, unplayed out material, for us. The outcome is, fundamentally, a problem of the ecology, albeit at a psychic level.

The new rule might read thus: our understanding of neurosis, of breakdown at this psychic level, of dysfunction, has been elaborated in what are little more than the adult games of knowledge of analytic disciplines and therapies. These constructions exist in conditional and

---

[51] Andrew Samuels, Bani Shorter and Fred Plaut (1987), *A Critical Dictionary of Jungian Analysis,* RKP, London

[52] Russell Meares (1993), *The Metaphor of Play,* Aronson Inc, Northvale, NJ USA

secondary states of being; they speak of rules, of competence and, finally, of conformity. We 'sublimate' to their supposed, healing realities. They are essentially ego-structured. The ludic, is not conformative of the ego, it is the realm of the Self. True well-being requires a re-acquaintance with that original state of play we encountered as a child. Not an infantile return, this is not some 'inner child' fundamentalism, but in a mature encounter with *lila*, play of the gods, as a consciousness of the Self. A Self-Realisation, in which:

> *'The concept of human existence as a life-and-death struggle for survival gives way to a new image of life as a manifestation of the cosmic dance or divine play.'* [53]

## Finally

> *'On how to sing*
> *the frog school and the skylark school*
> *are arguing'*

The Japanese poet Shiki captures in the tolled syllables of the haiku a debate which is central to our attitudes to play and peace. Until now our understanding of the ludic seems to have been limited to the external and more obvious elements of its essential characteristics. Hence we see play as the measurement of a contact with the world, through manipulation, mastery, movement and all the running, jumping activity of it all and as the ambit, merely, of the child. We adults live largely in ignorance of its spiritual dimension.

Little attention has been paid to the deeper, more latent strata of ludic energy. The underlying *numen* has been left unstated, ignored and abandoned. There is no trend energetically to fuel it, no ludic party to promote it, no fundamentalists, other than the play literate, to evangelise it. Our children are left solely to advance the cause. But it could be other. Together we could present play as having a recondite, spiritual meaning, relevant not only to children but to all of us. The essential stuff of play, is in reality, a pervading, bonding union of internal psychic material and our external, everyday existence. In short, play as an active, original, meditative source. Like Zen, play as akin to *wu wei,* the state of supreme ease and spontaneity due to being in complete attunement with the Tao:[54] a wordless, ecological *dharma.* Playgrounds could stand as *temenos*, sacred enclosures, for just such enactments.

The contemplation of this ludic eco-system requires adults to expose a vulnerability that we have unwilling, hitherto, to explore. It involves an interplay where we respect the child as an equal, or even a leader. Shaftsbury's cry that we 'must educate our masters' nowadays has a

---

[53] Stanislav Grof (1985), *Beyond the Brain,* State University of New York Press, New York, USA

[54] John Lash (1990), *The Seekers Handbook*, Harmony Books. New York, USA

deeper and more profound implication. The child might respond by saying they must re-educate those who have been their masters. That a significant part of this re-education has been going on in our playgrounds for thirty or forty years may come as a surprise to many. The result, and it is just discernable in its earliest forms, is a new description of play and the ludic, as an inner micro-ecology that mirrors macro-ecology, in a holographic consciousness. One that may help make us, 'if not at home, at least alertly, answerably peregrine in the unhousedness of the human circumstance.' [55] Stanislav Grof, offers:

> 'While the traditional model of psychiatry and psychoanalysis is strictly personalistic and biographical, modern consciousness research has added new levels, realms, and dimensions and shows the human psyche as being essentially commensurate with the whole universe and all existence.' [56]

William Blake takes a friend to a window and pointing to some children at play says, 'That is Heaven.' This heaven is not at some remove from us, it is the internal communion with our deepest sense of play. It occurs, in what Rilke maintained, was the 'innocence of always being a beginner', or Baudelaire's 'immaculate naivety'. The Biblical quotation that Eliade cites from Isaiah contains the delicate aphorism, 'the little child shall lead them' (Isaiah II: 6.); a matter that I am compelled to see as having profound environmental ramifications. Can we make ourselves more open to this kind of relationship as a ludic way of peace? Our ecological amity may depend on just such mature surrender.

> 'We stand at the gates of an important epoch, a time of ferment, when a new spirit moves forward in a new leap, transcends its previous shape and takes on a new one. All the mass of previous representations, concepts and bonds linking our world together are dissolving and collapsing like a dream picture. A new phase of the spirit is preparing itself. Philosophy especially has to welcome it, while others, who oppose it, impotently cling to the past.' [57]

**Gordon Sturrock**
March 1997

---

[55] George Steiner (1991), *as cited*

[56] Michael Talbot (1991), *The Holographic Universe,* Grafton Books, London

[57] G Hegel, as quoted by Francis Fukuyama (1992), *The End of History and the Last Man,* Penguin Books, London

# Managing Personal Behaviour – a View of Reflective Playwork

Perry Else

## Introduction

Play work currently faces many challenges. There has been a growing shift in the level of adult control over the lives of children. Some of this control, while exhorted in order to help keep children safe, may in fact lead to deeper long term problems with the child. Play work training appears to be focusing on the external behaviours apparent in play to the detriment of the personal and private dialogue between child and adult. This informal dialogue is where the best work has often been done, yet it has been facilitated by 'natural' playworkers and is in danger of being excluded from formal play work training as it develops. Reflective playwork, based in a therapeutic context, where workers are aware of and manage their own contribution to the play experience, offers an opportunity for play workers to move on to becoming people to be treasured for the skills and insight they can bring to a child's development.

## Some Working Definitions

Play is a process of learning about yourself, your identity in relation to your community and the world around you. It is the main process by which all human beings learn a sense of self, controlling their minds, their bodies and then those around them. Through play children also learn about the world and the elements within it, though it is recognised that not all children have the chance to achieve balance and expertise in these skills.

Children at the earliest age explore themselves and their environment, learning about textures, tastes, sights and sounds. As they begin to move around, they learn gross physical skills through crawling, walking, running and jumping. They then refine these through 'micro movements' into painting, writing and other creative skills, where there is an overlap between the physical world and the need to express their own inner world.

At the same time as developing physical skills, children will be learning social skills through interaction primarily with their mother figure and then the wider circle of care givers. A child given a healthy introduction to social life, which involves the mother figure in sharing and then expanding actions with the child, will gain a sense of self and self esteem that will enable them to function effectively in society. As the sense of mental agility is experienced, the development of identity is enhanced through social interaction, imagination, story-telling, drama and music. Russell Meares in his excellent book *The Metaphor of Play* goes further:

> '...the play of the pre-school child, and a mental activity similar to it in the adult, is necessary to the growth of a healthy self ...the play

*of the child is not mere diversion. It is vital to the evolution of mature psychic life.'* [58]

Play is best when it is freely chosen and its focus is directed by the player, whether consciously or unconsciously. David Wood explains:

*'Piaget through his theories of child development argues that the foundations of mental processes lie in action – 'thought is internalised action' ...children have to be active and constructive in order to develop their understanding of the world. Children who have not yet developed their mental abilities cannot examine experiences logically.*

*...Vygotsky argues that the capacity to learn through instruction is in itself a fundamental feature of human intelligence – when adults help children to accomplish things that they are unable to achieve alone, they are fostering the development of knowledge and ability.'* [59]

Either approach requires that the child co-operates or desires to repeat experiences (in order to learn through their actions). If the child is not willing to play because of lack of choice or a sense of being 'told what to do', development cannot occur. This assessment is being supported by the recent work of Gerald Edelman.

Edelman is beginning to show that the brain learns through a process of 'natural selection'. The brain (and so the child) needs diversity, interaction and choice if it is to develop – it is not a computer waiting for an instruction from an external programmer:

*'For Edelman, the brain is a generator of new behaviour. It reacts to the world in a totally unique way, motivated by its own system of values. If you substitute the word 'person' for the word 'brain', that statement is a summary of the idea of individual freedom of action. For Edelman, we are our brains, and because of this, we must construct our own version of the world. We are, in a sense, constrained to be free.'* [60]

For children, the free choice and focus of play is literally the chance to develop into a functioning, balanced adult. However, one of the ways that play is currently being constrained is through play environments.

## Current Concerns

Play environments are spaces where play is supported and encouraged. More and more, these environments come under the external control of authorities that limit the choice and diversity available to children. 'Authorities' affecting children will be culturally defined, but from a western context this means parental, adult, governmental and statutory authority.

---

[58] Russell Meares (1992), *The Metaphor of Play*, Hill of Content, Melbourne, Australia

[59] David Wood (1988), *How children think and learn*, Blackwell, Oxford UK

[60] David Sington et al (1994), *The man who made up his mind*, BBC, London UK

In recent times, parents have grown to fear other people and the built environment. This fear, whether real or perceived, when directed as instructions to children on how and where they can play, limits the child's interaction with a range of potential stimuli in the environment. As stated above, the parental influence is critical to the child's healthy development. But parental authority is becoming obsessed with keeping children 'safe' to the point where they can become developmentally harmed by being denied the freedom and opportunity to experiment and learn.

Parents are also beginning to question their own fitness to be parents and so we find the modern phenomenon of some children who are bought everything to play with yet are denied the very thing they most need – sensitive and responsive interaction. In short, there is a concern with the conditions of play manifest in the physical environment, and less so with the internal landscape. And yet, as Winnicott suggests:

> *'From birth … the human being is concerned with the problem of the relationship between what is objectively perceived and what is subjectively conceived of, and in the solution to the problem there is no health for the human being who has not been started off well enough by the mother.'* [61]

Similarly, other adults have come to see themselves and others as dangerous to children. Not very long ago, the community had a sense of the 'extended family' where all the members would care for young people. As society has moved away from collective to individual responsibilities, people have generally given up their sense of care for the young and in its place have become more aware of their own 'right' to live without being 'bothered' by young people. This has led to a situation where children and young people are frequently seen as 'problems' being denied the chance to play spontaneously; the evidence of this is provided almost daily in the press and on TV.

It is also true that there has been a loss of authority and respect for people who have had a responsibility (albeit informally) for the well being of children – teachers, park-keepers, caretakers and the police. The breakdown in socially accepted barriers of behaviour has led to further and further developments of anti-social and dysfunctional behaviour.

Governmental authority has also changed the environments for children to play in. Local government influenced by central government has implemented highway and street design that has limited the opportunity for people without transport to move around, and this has especially affected children and young people. Authority, not law, has also affected how children should play in parks and playgrounds. Fears of safety, at a time when local government budgets have been reduced, have led to many reductions in play spaces and play equipment in

---

[61] DW Winnicott, 1991, *Playing and Reality*, Penguin, London UK

municipal parks. The report *Park Life* by Comedia Demos [62] (1995), while highlighting what we have lost, strongly makes the case for parks as public spaces and as valuable cultural crucibles.

However fears of safety have also affected legislation – in England, this has chiefly come through the Children Act 1989. This Act, drawn up with the intention of putting children first, is leading to an increase in care provision and a decline in play provision.

Again these changes have been brought in without adequate resources to implement them. The pressures of registering all provision for children under eight years have forced some informally ran, but generally safe, play schemes to close. And perversely, a review is considering taking some provisions out of the remit of the Act rather than have them 'brought up to standard' to meet its current requirements. The Children Act also had an effect on play workers in that there are pressures for them to meet an agreed standard of provision and become assessed as a registered worker.

Play workers are people working in play environments whose role is to support and encourage play. Increasingly this support includes an element of care for the safety and well being of the child. The Children Act has now made care for children under eight a statutory requirement in playwork, and professional initiatives such as the National Vocational Qualifications have also led to play work being seen as a series of tasks that correctly implemented will result in a 'safe and happy' child. In the need to meet the concerns of external authorities, workers have taken on these concerns and set out to make play 'safe' – an impossible goal.

### Early Years Awareness – a Vital Consideration

It is against this background of concerns to do with changing perceptions of children and worker's personal safety that the focus on the quality of play has arisen. It is my contention that true play work is more interesting and more complicated than is generally recognised – just as the flavour of wine is more than grapes grown in soil, mashed and then fermented, so children are more complex than is recognised under the current system. The focus in play work at the moment is upon the external behaviours and processes of play, hence the urge to define and categorise activities that produce 'safe play'. The thought processes and internal behaviours of both the child at play and the playworker are much more significant to the whole development process, yet they are rarely considered in the play work field.

To quote Winnicott again:

> '...I am concerned with the search for the self and the restatement of the fact that certain conditions are necessary if success is to be achieved in this search. These conditions are associated with what is usually

---

[62] L Greenhaigh and Ken Walpole, 1995, *Park Life – Urban Parks and social renewal*, Comedia Demos, Stroud & London UK. Section V, 'Park life today'

*called creativity. It is in playing and only in playing that the individual child or adult is able to be creative and to use the whole personality, and it is only in being creative that the individual discovers the self.'* [63]

It has been recognised for many years that the early years' development of children is critical to their mental and physical maturity. This period is in the main the time when parents and family carers have traditionally had most access to the child. There is a growing recognition of the need for quality nursery provision for all children to offset the imbalance caused by the change in traditional family roles, yet this is by no means a universal provision in England. In their early years, a child literally learns the patterns that will shape their mind and their life. Children need access to diversity, interaction and choice or they potentially become dysfunctional in later life. Breaks in support from the mother figure or primary carer can lead to children feeling 'a sense of unease, a fear which is like teetering on the edge of a void'. When this figure repeatedly 'fails to make adequate responses to the experiences of the child, the child will be left with a diminished sense of the reality and meaning of his or her existence'. [64]

However, play workers have intuitively recognised their importance in working with children. Workers have seen themselves in an informal therapeutic role, helping children come to grips with the world, by being a mature friend. This was helped by the fact that play work has generally been outside of school (after school or in holidays) where children's freedom to play has been (if not respected then at least) allowed and encouraged. It is in the shift towards 'professionalism' (through gaining qualifications) and in the fear of being blamed for putting children at risk (through the Children Act), that the play field has become concerned about processes; with the omission of the most vital part – the personal and private dialogue between child and adult.

This omission has come about because play workers have generally not had any formal training in this very vital part of their tool kit. Traditional play training focuses on child facilitation skills, play skills, administration, health and safety, personal organisation. In the NVQ, and stressed to differing degrees in other qualifications, is the need for 'underpinning knowledge'. An awareness of child development is mentioned as knowledge necessary to 'run through' a worker's practice. Yet it is usually the area of a course syllabus that is given short shrift when compared to the 'rules of games' or 'how to organise a day trip out'.

Of course I am not arguing that these competencies are not valuable, but without a clear understanding of the role of play in children's lives, these skills can simply be diversionary activities that do not deal with the underlying developmental issues. Playwork education needs the balance necessary to inform our practice, so that the tacit therapeutic role playworkers take is more informed and better understood. This balance

---

[63] DW Winnicott, (1991), As cited

[64] Russell Meares (1992), As above

would then help in aiding playworkers move on from being the informal counsellors mentioned above, to being adults who have a critical role to play in the continuing development of children and young people. When playworkers are seen as people to be treasured for the skills and insight they can bring to a child's development, our status and standing will change dramatically.

## A Re-definition of Playwork Practice

Critical to this change is recognising that play workers have choices, they can intervene in children's activity or not. Intervention may be justified in socially accepted terms – to stop fighting, to challenge racism, to help a child make a better product (e.g. mask, kite or pancake) – but intervention is still a control exerted by one person over another. The issue is how *conscious* this control is to the worker. (What we call reflective playwork is an awareness of this possibility of control.)

Many relationships in our current times have become power relationships – one person is in charge, the other subservient. And, with the current fears about safety, are workers still confident about using their own judgements, secure in the knowledge that they can answer any criticism from others?

Play workers need to play several roles in their work – friend, supporter, teacher, police officer. The easiest role is that of police officer, but in addition to direction, children at times need coaching, supporting and friendship.

Better play workers find these roles easy to put on and take off; in effect they are entering into a play world with the children they work with. Most of us play different roles daily; assertive at work, passive with at home with our children, aggressive in the car! Playwork, as part of a reflective and analytic practice, involves being aware of these roles and the messages they give to children.

At times this will involve the worker directing the child, at other times, the child will be directing the worker. Additionally, in our current practice, children will not often have the luxury of one-to-one interaction with a worker, so that the messages and interaction may not be the most appropriate to what a particular child needs *at that moment*. We need the awareness that enables us to pick up the clues that children send to us through their play, and the time and resources to respond appropriately.

In play, the child may or may not be aware of the relationship; they are playing, they want to see 'what happens if…' Children will want to explore boundaries; they will want to push workers to see what develops.

Good (or perhaps better) workers will play roles yet will always be in control of themselves; a children's play environment is not the best place for adults to let themselves go – there are adult playgrounds where this is more socially acceptable. In controlling themselves they are able to judge when to intervene in play. They will let play develop without intervention until their own 'conscience' or the rules of the authority controlling the play environment tell them someone is going too far. Rules are easy to follow and so become comfortable. But if we use our judgement, what about 'conscience' where does it come from, can it be trusted? Better play workers will be aware that their conscience is a pattern learned from their society and will question their own decisions through reflection and evaluation. We are becoming better as a group in immediately questioning statements that prejudice women, people from different cultures and people with disabilities. We still have a lot to learn about 'common sense', the informal education our own culture ingrains in us. For example, and relevant to this debate, is how we learn to think about power relationships and our society's current obsession with 'safety'.

In playwork we currently speak of 'reflective practice'. We are encouraged to look back at the day and learn from it – what went well, what didn't go so well and what we would change. Without an awareness of what is guiding our decisions and debates *in the moment*, we are in danger of 'post event rationalisation' – we see the event as a one-off happening dictated by circumstances 'beyond our control' and so justify our behaviour in terms of how we reacted (or didn't react).

Most interventions will be concerned with safety (trying to prevent harm to self or others) or with learning (helping someone to see other less harmful ways to change situations; e.g., by negotiating rather than fighting). Yet we need to be aware that by intervening we may be projecting our thoughts and judgements onto the situation, and therefore changing the outcome and perception of what was happening.

For instance, children in their rough and tumble play often have an unwritten code of what is fair and acceptable behaviour. Being allowed to play roughly lets them learn how to control their bodies and emotions; they learn that fighting hurts and may develop a sense of choice in participating in violent acts. Children denied the chance to 'fight' when young may learn to fantasise about fighting and death in an unreal and harmful way.

## Summary

Reflective playwork allows us to respect ourselves and therefore have respect for children. If a worker respects the child's right to play, they will not casually intervene or 'manage' that play. If that worker feels the play is becoming inappropriate for that play environment, they will intervene showing concern and respect for the child. The child may then learn from the experience rather than simply putting it down to yet another adult shouting at them and telling them what to do. Children may learn for themselves through information and choice – rather than responding to a worker through fear. The worker should also be able to learn something about themselves and so will extend their own development and understanding. This continuum of leadership and sharing is a two-way street that is crucial to our work in play.

By evaluating themselves, being aware of and reflecting on their own behaviours and the relationships they create, play workers can effectively manage themselves and be positively involved in a child's playing experience, creating space for both to grow and discover their individual selves.

**Perry Else**
April 1997

# Child X as a Case History

Gordon Sturrock

*'Don't play what's there, play what's not there.'*

Miles Davis

## Example of child X

*Example of child X:*

He always starts well, comes in good form. He gets bored, has a short attention span. He finds it difficult to wait to get involved in a game etc.

When he flips without warning

He hits other children

Uses bad language

Steals

There is one boy he gets on especially badly with. He spends a lot of time on his own.

*What volunteers do:*

Tell him to stop

Go into 'one to one' – i.e. take him aside to do something else

If you give him attention he's alright

He is sometimes asked to leave. [65]

This initial outline represents in an abbreviated form a kind of classic, 'set situation'. It is my intention to provide a process of analysis of the behaviours and to outline a methodology out of which the playworker can examine and understand their reactions and responses. In short, to attempt to explicate what might properly be described as 'reflective' playwork practice. It should be noted that though the authorship of this article is my own that the ideas and work out of which it is drawn has been in conjunction with my colleagues Stephen Rennie and Bob Hughes.

I must first offer a warning. This approach is at odds with much of what constitutes the present background to our understanding of play and the child within the play setting. It reverses key elements of what we hold to be true of playwork. In addition, as some of the methods and techniques are borrowed from the depth psychologies (that is, analytical psychology and psychoanalysis), from a variety of therapies, and from my own recollections of playwork experience, the language and

---

[65] Bob Hughes (1996), as quoted from, *Reflective Analytic Playwork in Northern Ireland*, training notes, PlayEducation, Ely, Cambs. UK

48

conceptual basis for the approach are sometimes difficult and often personal.

I have one further caveat to put. What I propose here is, naturally, at a distance from the actual exchanges that the particular playworker or volunteer went through/is going through with this child, I am attempting merely to suggest a form which will allow the expression and reflections for what those who work with Child X undergo, to let it have some meaning, to suggest that almost every playworker has a 'Child X' in their play experience. But, inevitably, my thoughts at a remove from the action.

I would like at this stage, to outline two points or attitudes and a methodological framework which. in my view, will help us in our understanding of the essential dynamics and Interchanges lying at the heart of Child X's expressive acts. What might be termed his *dysplay.*

> The first element of our approach is that we are required to reverse the usual objective/subjective status which pertains when we interact with others. In playwork, we are required to be subjective, not about ourselves, but about the children with whom we work. That is, we are required to put aside certain desires of our own in service of the process of the child's play. There is a common failure which occurs in playwork practice where the unfulfilled play desires of the adult playworker/volunteer come to dominate the play agenda on sites and locations. I can date many adventure playgrounds where the carefully designed and built structures were actually too good for the children to play on and where the playworker was primarily concerned with their prestige and standing rather than as the locus of children's play. We might see this process as an adulteration of play.

> Our objectivity should extend to our own relationship with the playing child. We are required both to be an integral part of the child's play and to have the ability to set it into frames and to re-frame it objectively. This objectivity about ourselves means that we can have, for example, an affinity with the child or children, meeting their moods, without losing a perspective on our work. We can empathise with their joy and their rages without becoming overjoyed or raging ourselves.

The methodology is a little more difficult to state easily and may require an unpacking but I would sum it up thus: If, as Igvar Jonansen, suggests:

> '*All behaviour is performed and learned in specific environments in relationship to specific behaviour-contingent events… what is learned is not a behaviour pattern but a* behaviour-environment-event *pattern.*' (My emphasis)

Then this *behaviour-environment-event* pattern is one that has a ready application to the process of play. But, as it stands it is not entirely sufficient. I would add one further elaboration to the procedural description to make it wholly contingent with our playwork practice. This concerns, as James Hillman's states, that part of the growth of what we might understand as the Self, our essential identity, our soul, which rests in our capacity to deepen events into experiences. He says:

> *'Because our psychic stuff is images, image-making is a* via regia, *a royal road to soul-making. The making of soul-stuff calls for dreaming, fantasying, imagining. To live psychologically means to imagine things: to be in touch with soul means to live in sensuous connection with fantasy. To be in soul, is to experience the fantasy in all realities and the basic reality of fantasy.'*

As this has such pertinence to the ludic dimension of the child's life, could so readily be descriptive of the play function, in evaluating our responses within these patterns I believe we are required to add this dimension to Johansson's initial articulation. Hillman, an analytical psychologist, talks of that 'unknown component which makes meaning possible, turns events into experiences'. I would advocate that when we reflectively respond to our lifeworld, enter the event patterning I outline, we have another layer or level of consideration which we bring to bear. This is – as a definition of the reflective objectivity that we as playworkers bring to bear in our practice – that we take into account the field of experience from which we trawl our responses: of our own childhood, our recalled play experiences, our histories, what Freud described as the 'family romance', our love and our work; all experience that was met as well as those which were thwarted.

Now, the behaviour-environment-event pattern has an additional component, that of experience. That of our past and the present experience we share with the child/children. So the formula now reads *behaviour-environment-event-experience* pattern.

Let's return to Child X and begin to apply the methodology. We might view the following summary as a 'problem' to which I suggest that we apply not so much a solution but a process which will allow a resolution to be tested against the description of the problem. Hence the 'set situation' can be utilised as a tutelatory example.

The script, I use that term advisedly, which X offers us seems at first glance to be fairly straightforward. He arrives and is 'in good form,' his behaviour for whatever reason deteriorates, he behaves in ways which are inappropriate, resulting in either his being accommodated or expelled. Let's apply the formula

## Behaviour

Child X arrives at the playground with an unconscious agenda that he is compelled to express. For the main part this would appear to be anger. It is worth noting that his anger, is initially at least, suppressed. This allows us to speculate that it is also suppressed elsewhere in his life. On the play site it takes him over. So, while it is useful to categorise the behaviour as hitting, stealing and so on, it is not sufficiently descriptive of the compulsion which is being enacted. Child X demonstrates that he is in the grip of what in other fields is denoted as *'affect'*. A useful quick definition of affect is that is emotion which functions beyond will. That is to say that no matter what constraints X attempts to put on his outward demeanour a deeper more latent need takes over.

In addition, it appears that his ability to enter into games, (for games I suggest that we remind ourselves that games are play with rules) is incomplete. He is bored quickly and has a short attention span. An almost classic description of what used to be called 'hyperactivity' and what is now referred to as Attention Deficit Disorder, or ADD. Now, the interesting thing about ADD is that while it is a much recorded and observed disorder, there exist a huge variety of renderings and treatments, some involving regimes of drugs.

The account which I and my colleagues favour, out of our play experiences, runs as follows. Though play has in the literature been described as a behaviour this is erroneous. Play is a drive as much as hunger or sex is. Our research into ADD has shown, that in many cases, children arrive at the play centre of whatever type and fire off *play cues* to the environment. For the many, these play cues are picked up by their friends, other children, the workers/volunteers and so on. As the play cue is met, and indeed in good play habitats is encouraged and re-enforced, healthy play ensues. For the few, they too fire off play cues which are not picked up. They then have to cope with these cues returning to them unmet. The cues are then re-issued – this is material which must be brought out and played with for it to be safely reordered and understood – and are now laden with anxiety which tends to abreact with others in play. This cycle then repeats *ad nauseam.* Eriksson's idea that: 'The play construction, then, can be seen to be inventively negotiating between the small builder's inner universe and his society's changing world view', is particularly apposite and would show that in the construction of their lifeworld, these children could already be marked apart, as solitary and unheeded.

The child with whom X has a particular antipathy may well be successful at the play interactions which he himself finds so difficult. The exclusion (the derivation of that word has the root lu*dic* and effectively means out of play) is merely his responding to what is internally in process, namely; that he feels excluded! Where he expects to be rejected, he responds by getting his rejection in first. His lifeworld script is that of rejection and exclusion and is already well established. That having been said, the playground still offers a place where he can work, or more significantly, play through these intense personal dramas. In my view, the likelihood is that for many children in the thrall of such compulsions, the playground and the playworker, of whatever status, represent the only place where the child's problem is encountered, enacted and where in their judgement lies the potential to cure.

## Environment

I would like to make one general point about the environmental factors which contribute to this particular problem. There is a widely held perception which suggests that the adult is somehow the more 'sophisticated' partner in the child/adult relationship, the child is the more 'primitive'. This attitude certainly prevails in those disciplines to which playwork has been likened such as teaching, youth work and so on. The core of their ethos is the transmission of learning or conditioning. They would contend that they are the sophisticated holders of values or knowledge imparting them to primitive unformed children. This is not the case in playwork. While other professions see themselves as preoccupied with the transmission of truth, we in playwork may be involved in the co- formation of 'healing fictions'.

The irony is that in playwork it is we adults who have had our play potentiality enclosed by our various undertakings. As Gide suggests, to make a choice is to lose an experience; by age, by acculturisation, by custom and habit, by marriage and mortgage. It is the child who exists in a sophisticated range of playful, 'as-if' potentiality. If I as a 48 year-old contemplate becoming an astronaut I am forced to consider my experience of other such weighty tasks, the child can do so instantly.

The same edict applies to the very forms of setting within which we work. Paradoxically, the more advanced and established the play setting the more primitive it will be in the variety of environmental factors which need to be taken into accounts of its practice. The more short-term, or short-lived, the less well resourced, the more voluntary (and so on), the greater is the complexity and sophistication of dynamics that intrude on the play space and the adult/child relationships therein.

The interesting thing about X's outbursts, even though they are affective and have some aspects of unconscious behaviour, is that one key element should clearly be understood. This is, that X's rage happens in a place which he knows to be safe. He seeks the containment of the playground/site to express his dis-ease. While we can argue in the issuing and return of the driven play cues that containment is necessary – other children at the play centre I am sure have the play cycle of driven material, cue, containment, return and re-issue, satisfactorily met – X's drive requires a larger stage and a different language of response. So unsure – is untrusting a better term – is he, that his play will be understood or met, that he controls the script, albeit unconsciously, so that the anxiety-laden, enraged cues he issues are greeted by one-to-one exchanges where they will not be lost, or misunderstood, or ignored. The dynamic procedure of abreaction/response is steadily being ritualised. X demands his rites. Indeed, so powerful is this demand that he now commands a stage where I am involved some many hundred miles away and where his play cues will be the focus of attention of a large group he has never met!

52

To paraphrase and re-order a little Bob Hughes' definitional states of environments, I would say that the play environment is controlled by X to ensure that it responds in a way which he most readily understands. In short, X demands a negative environment for him to thrive in the only way he knows how. All of which begs the question: *if the playground is acting as a compensatory ground for this behaviour, what is active elsewhere which prompts this dysplay?* It could be said, with degrees of certainty, that the playground environment and the staff are engaged in the prophylactic containment of projected material which X feels it would be unsafe to unload in other situations and circumstances.

## Event

In the last section I spoke of the ritualisation of behaviour which can happen in the play environment. Part of the drive to play may seek the safety of containment of ritual; X's right to rite. An example out of my own experience may have some relevance.

Our problem was of an older boy who had outgrown the site and provision and who could not be weaned away from the playground. The effect, due to his physical maturity and oversize needs, was the constant disruption of other, younger children's, playing. Our response, after many misses, was to create a highly ritualised farewell ceremony with wildly exaggerated, content, speeches, responses and farewells into which all the children fell with some glee. The upshot was that a difficult right of passage for our young man was safely and soothingly negotiated. From then on his less frequent appearances on the playground were in the form of an adult and mature demeanour.

The same might be said of the responses made to X's demanding stances. The outcomes, even in the brief description offered, have a curious form, almost like some dyadic dance. The results of his behaviour, his 'reward,' is either that his play needs are met, or that he is banished. Either way they there is an 'event' which he can translate or understand. While this may be the case, within the over-dramatic stage of X's dysplay, it is more particularly true of children's play generally. Here the playworker is involved in a variety of play narratives, dramas, passages which they move in-and-out of in the course of their everyday work. In each of these exchanges lies the potential to create an 'event'. These can vary from the minuscule to the momentous, the point being that in each case we as playworkers are required to be sensitive to our role in the event and the overall pattern of *behaviour-environment-event* potentiality. Some play may need little fanfare and tiny gestures, even down to a nod and a wink; others may require more elaborate flounces and flourishes. (As an aside, in the longer term, it might be useful for playworkers to trace the importance of 'event' as rite, ritual and ceremony, as it is explicated and understood in anthropology and ethnology to enhance our understanding of our practice. I have long argued that there are clear parallels between the work of the shaman, the medicine man or woman, and that of the worker active in play.)

The event of the play cycle is that point where we are drawn into the loop of the child's play, as a resource, as a role player, as an umpire for judgements, for comfort, we can all add to this list. This intervention, at whatever level, requires us to be sensitive to the origins of the play that is going on and to which we have to adapt. We must also ensure that we leave the scene as intact as we can manage. The adult world is not as tolerant of the deconstructive side of creativity any more than it is play. We are burdened not to adulterate the child's play with our internal and adult needs for preservation. By making an event we leave a marker of our own presence on that part of the child's play with which we have had contact. This marker leaves a trace which may be lasting. However, at the level of the event these imprints are less significant than those we may leave at the next strata: that of experience.

## Experience

Much of what I have written here thus far is an acknowledgement of parts of our task which are obvious, even if stated in different terms. The deepening of the event into an experience is a more difficult and abstract proposition.

When I question my own play, I can resurrect fragments which have over years accumulated layers of meaning for me. The writer John Fowles gives a useful example:

> 'When I was a child my Cornish grandmother told me that the pure white husks I sometimes found in the jetsam along the shore were the souls of drowned sailors: and some such concrete image as this of countless centuries of folk-belief has remained in all of us, even though intellectually we know what I discovered about the cuttle-bones: that eventually they go yellow and crumble into dust.'

I am no longer sure whether some tales have any resemblance to an actuality, I am unsure that they are real. They have transcended that description because they have become laden with meaning. They have a kind of 'bejewelled' quality. That this might also be true for others is confirmed on the odd occasions when I meet adults who were children on playgrounds I worked on twenty years or more ago. I am greeted by their recall of incidents which seem to me to be commonplace but which to them have precisely the quality I have described. Events have for them been deepened into experiences.

Child X appears to have an intensified need to ensure that this deepening of the event into an experience takes place. He insists that the humdrum event of intervention be dramatised and surrounded by the potentiality to experience. Ordinary play eludes him or is sidelined by his greater need for meaning. It is worth noting that this meaning, which for children can often be conveyed by their peers or elders, is held. It would seem, only by the adult. X, like many children, lures the playworker to cross a threshold from an externalised play into play which exists in an internalised and perhaps secret place. Though this is not the time to discuss more fully this precious and dangerous crossing over we can highlight one crucial aspect of our work in this area.

Children are surrounded by those who have an adult interest in their lives. The greater number of their elders – from siblings, other older children, their families, to the many professionals involved in their development – are chiefly concerned with their induction into society. That is a worthy enough aim but it should be understood that this happens almost entirely according to the mores and demands of an adult society. Playworkers suggest something other.

We stand as mediators between the child and the adult both in terms of the preservation of the right to play, the actual space and the play that goes on within it, and in decoding and translating the content of the most intimate and internalised play of the child's inner world; what Manley Hopkins described as an 'Inscape'. When we enter into this 'inscape' we cannot leave the baggage of our own adulthood, our experience, at the door. We enter intact, and, we above all, must ensure that we understand precisely what impression we leave at this point of contact *from our own content.* If a child should make a disclosure, whether real or imagined, we are burdened with the need to treat it as it stands for that child without the addition of projected material from our own past. I have personal experience of a child who told a playworker a secret of incest which then triggered the worker's own incest memory. In this case the child's was imagined, the worker's was real. The untangling of the two was fraught with difficulty.

I use this example to illustrate a point but the ethos which is hinted at – of strictly limited contamination – applies to the most mundane aspects of play. We sit at the confluence of one of the most profound experiences that the child can undertake. We ought to bear in mind that play is not simply a behaviour which can be changed and altered to suit prevailing trends and circumstances. Play is a drive. We are compelled to play. Play is not merely a precursor to education, to induction into society. It is the essence of all learning. It is the *prefiguring element* of all creativity.

The work of the eminent psychiatrist Russell Meares has been described as using:

> '...the field of play to cast a bright light on the developmental ontogeny of the sense of self. He describes in depth the characteristics of the child and caregiver relations by which enduring patterns are laid down that subsequently provide the fateful core of self experience.'

It is within this web of relationships, of the most crucial, formative kind, where the work of play begins. It is in service of these tentative and difficult interactions that the dynamic processes of the work take shape. Playgrounds, playworkers and children all interact to create containers of meaning for the playing child, moment-to-moment, day-to-day. To borrow a term from depth psychology, in play, we also work at the level of the *psychic.* As such, it could be argued that play and playwork functions in preventing the formation of longer-term, neurotic complexes. It is therefore difficult to imagine playwork where this therapeutic contact is avoided. Child X proves the need.

Entry to the internal experiential realm also means that playworkers too become marked and touched by the contact. Our working practice as it stands at the moment has no means where these exchanges can be re-examined, and, if need be, exorcised. That this reflection is not built into our practice and remains somewhat extra-mural to our job descriptions does a disservice not just to our desire for professional standing but also to the task of working with children. Some believe that it is not the purpose of playwork to deal with these issues. The question remains: then who does? In a real sense playworkers may encounter these problems, this dis-ease, at their formation; should we not be equipped to treat them?

Where we encounter what we have termed *dysplay* we see clear signs and signals that there is an already operative breakdown in this adaptive, ludic behaviour. There is a great danger that we exclude just those who are establishing innate patterns of disruptive play, and, resulting, societal dis-ease. In a cruel accord with more generalised practices of mental health, we return the traumatised to the streets. Those who show the greatest need are being denied access. This is not a task that playwork can deny.

## To Conclude

I am convinced that for each playworker there exist any number of 'Child Xs'. What becomes of them as they mature into adulthood? For a frightening clue is apparent. I am struck by the close parallels of description between a child labelled as having ADD, and that of an adult condition described in the literature of psychoanalysis as an intractable problem; namely, the 'borderline patient'. In a masterstroke of avoidance, Pontalls and Laplanche define the term 'borderline patient' as:

> '...most often used to designate psychopathological troubles lying on the frontier between neurosis and psychosis, particularly latent schizophrenias presenting an apparently neurotic set of symptoms.'

They then goes on to say 'this term has no nosographical definition' – that is it cannot be classified.

I have already suggested that the hyperactive child is firing off over-rapid play cues *which are not being met.* The circulating play energy returns and is then re-issued but this time with the burden of anxiety. A now angst-laden play cue is issued which is also not met and then returns in a vicious cycle of cue, unmet expression and return. The consequence of this unmet play need is the speeded-up behaviour, the short attention span and lack of concentration of the so-called hyperactive child. Perhaps X, reassured that the playworker was able to pick up his play cues and that she/he can enter into his internalised, imaginal, play fantasy in the one-to-one situation, begins to show signs of relaxation and reduction in apparent stress.

Two factors need therefore to be considered. Hyperactive behaviour may have some linkage with play activity and its functional environment. The anxiety of the hyperactive child may well be that they are in fact over-sensitive to the potentialities of what Winnicott calls the 'third area', the most internalised play realm, call it what you will, and as a consequence become anxious that others cannot enter so readily into this inner psychic play space. The combination of these factors results in the so-called hyperactive symptomology.

All of this leaves a further and intriguing speculation unexplored, one that arises from a statistic which states that some 60% of children named as ADD will go on to become adults who show some marked behavioural alteration. It is apparent from what I have thus far observed that there is a possibility of some initial correspondence between what has come to be understood (I hesitate to use word defined) as the borderline patient and the hyperactive child.

At the beginning of his work, 'The Metaphor of Play', Russell Meares affectingly describes the problem as one of those:

*'…who suffer a persuasive feeling of emptiness, who live as if on the surface, caught up in a ceaseless traffic with the stimuli of the everyday world… These people sense no core existence and are often without access to true emotions or an authentic feeling of being alive. Such disturbances of the experience of the self are common. Indeed, people afflicted with them make up the bulk of those who confront a psychotherapist in the modem age. Their severity ranges from a subtle and unobtrusive disturbance of personality, to a severely disabling condition associated with repeated hospitalisations, suicides attempts, and broken relationships.'*

Stan Mould, Founder and Chairman of LADDER (Learning, Hyperactivity and Attention Deficit Disorders Association) writes in the opening to Professor Eric Taylor's book, 'The Hyperactive Child':

*'In January 1992, my life had been pretty tough for a few years – I was 43, my marriage had broken up two years previously, another relationship had broken up nine months beforehand, I was having significant problems at work, and was drinking heavily and had few friends. Furthermore, my just fourteen-year-old son's school reports had deteriorated to a level where the school and I were seriously concerned. Strangely, the things they were saying about him were echoes of what was said about me – things like if only he'd concentrate', 'why can't he sit still', 'he distracts everyone else', 'doesn't he ever listen' Indeed, they still were being said about me.'*

Both of these statements and quotes contain more than the echo of hyperactivity. They also echo each other. They speak in the same affective modality. They begin, at least in my mind, to raise the question: is the hyperactive child the borderline adult? Could play be curative? Is there room and validity for just such a psycholudic description of the problem? Might the treatment of the adult condition also have some potential for cure which is contained within the ludic, creative urges of childhood?

Almost every therapy contains some germ of play at the core of its therapeutic endeavours. If so, where does this place the work of the playworker who is unavoidably and intuitively operative in the same area? To follow the child's cues and enter into an internalised, constructed fantasy with them, may be (in addition to the greatest care we can give a child) a prime source of our well-being as humankind. Play is the energetic expression of a profound internal ecology. One, into which we are invited by the child. The Greek word, *therapeia* (from which we derive our term therapy) meant to 'be in service of the gods'. It is in the service of the child's gods at play that playwork should focus its attention. If so, it is worth considering for playwork a definitional background such as that which the child psychoanalyst Winnicott proposes, namely, that;

> 'It is play that is the universal, and that belongs to health: playing facilitates growth and therefore health; playing leads into group relationships: playing can be a form of communication in psychotherapy; and lastly, psychoanalysis has been developed as a highly specialised form of playing in the service of communication with oneself and others.'

My thanks to X and those who proposed the outline. My apologies for any liberties which may have been taken.

**Gordon Sturrock**
April 1996

# The Survival Self – an Analysis of the Effects of Survival in a Sectarian Environment

Gordon Sturrock
for Maeve McKee

Eta Halbschmerz, ein zwelter,
ohne Dauerspur, halbwegs
hier. Eine Halblust
Bewegtes, Beseteztes.

A half-pain, a second one, with
no lasting trace, halfway
here. A half-desire
things in motion, things
occupied.

Weiderholungszwangs-
Camaleu

Cameo
of compulsive repetition

Paul Celan

## Introduction

It might be useful, given what follows, to offer a brief introductory explanation to the ideas I take up here. This paper was written in answer to my own feelings in encountering the effects of the sectarian nature of life in Northern Ireland and is based on one central and unavoidable conclusion; namely, that sectarianism is rife and those who exist within its compass can only do so by the accommodation of its extremity through forms of co-optive adaption.

For those who live there, this adjustment and the explication of the costs of just such accommodation, has hitherto not been explored in terms of the individual and of the impact on the psyche, on aspects of internalised human development, on existential life. And, if the notable descriptions of the effects are solely in terms of the external outcomes, the sociological implications, and are as a result partial, then I argue that any ameliorating response will also be correspondingly partial. It is in an attempt to broaden the categories of damage that sectarianism entails and in an effort to outline a countering therapeutic strategy that I write this paper.

I must indicate that my stance is taken after the briefest of contacts – a two-day workshop on the Issue in Belfast and without recognisable authority – and it is from this somewhat detached perspective that I write. I was present at the workshop solely as a participant observer. Criticisms along these lines I therefore wholeheartedly acknowledge: nevertheless I feel obliged to continue. I owe a great debt of thanks to Bob Hughes, who introduced me to this area of interest and to the members of the aforementioned workgroup, all of whom I regard as co-authors of this paper and from whom I ask forgiveness for any liberties taken.

I intend to use some ideas from the depth psychologies, psychoanalysis and analytical psychology, without too much adherence to their schools, to develop a range of metaphors that describe the idea of a 'survival self'. It is the cost of maintenance of this 'survival self' that is the fundamental thrust of this essay.

## The False Self

During the course of the various exercises undertaken in the workshop, I was struck by the ability of participants to 'manage' what appeared to be the intractable, all-pervasive nature of sectarianism, as we discussed it. From the accounts of the group members. It would appear that the costs of such division to the community, that inevitably should be rendered communities given the location, is well understood. What is less well understood is the undoubted emotional cost of living and working in the sectarian climate. As an outsider to the situation, albeit one with a declared interest in therapeutic approaches, this seemed to be an area that was worthy of further elucidation. As this exploration was not appropriate, by the very nature of the group's constitution, at the time, I do so now by means of this paper.

I would like to use the working of the group and particular incidents and effects, seen from a thematic viewpoint, to begin to outline a functional formation that I regard as being of some import. The trigger, the moment of truth to dramatize my premise, came at a point when the group had been examining the implications of sectarianism for some three to four hours. We were all a little tired and to a certain extent defences, a word used advisedly, began to crumble. What we encountered, as an appreciable group phenomena, was a moment of marked depression. Energy levels plummeted, there was a lot of uneasy shifting and fidgeting, which I read as avoidance behaviour, and the dynamic and thrust of the workshop ground to a halt. The business of the group essentially stopped. There was a real, palpable and *felt* interregnum.

As the purpose of the workshop was not in any sense therapeutic – this was not an encounter group – after some efforts by Bob Hughes, the group's facilitator, to explain and work through this impasse, he rightly moved the group on to a more physical and practical exercise to conclude the work for that day. The next day, when we met again, and in recapitulating the last day's work, Bob raised the issue of this 'emotional blip', as I described It. As he did so the same pervasive feeling of heavy despondency and emotional repression filled the room. I felt it as a tangible presence. Bob, a very experienced group worker, asked with some considerable persistence, if the effect of sectarianism that the group felt, and its repression, was the cause. "Was this denial?" he asked. After a brief interchange where this inquiry remained posed but unresolved we moved on to other topics. However, the question still remains and I feel it necessary, not least for my own piece of mind, to attempt to essay an answer.

As a leitmotif I take two exchanges from the group that I would like to develop into an original explication of the impact of sectarianism. One group member, there were also others, had lived in England for a number of years. She spoke of that time as being a period where she felt a certain freedom of expression, she was more 'open and tolerant'. I asked her if she felt the same on her return to Northern Ireland, she said not. I briefly outlined Winnicott's idea of the 'false self' – I will develop this more fully later – and asked her in which location had she felt she had been her 'true self'. She was at first minded to reply Northern Ireland, but after some momentary reflection, she said that it had been in England. Another group member who had also lived on the mainland for many years had explained how, out of Northern Ireland, news from the province moved her to tears, a reaction that no longer occurred now that she was back. (These two narratives did not happen coincidentally, I simply bring them together for the purposes of my argument.)

From this admittedly slender evidence I would like to draw out an idea. As this will require delving into some psychoanalytic material and concepts and I hope you will bear with me. It is integral to the proposition I intend to make.

The psychoanalyst, D.W. Winnicott – whose work has an as yet little recognised significance for the work of play but who. given the context within which the workshop was taking place, is an appropriate authority – talks of the idea of the child developing what he describes as the 'false self'. I believe that this idea of the false self, at least as a metaphoric currency, provides a useful platform from which to explore the idea of sectarianism and its impact on the psyche and self identity. If I might explain.

I offer the following quotes as elucidations of his notion. Winnicott, and this was the definition that jolted me into this recognition, in a kind of synchronicity, describes the false self as a 'defence organisation' – I can think of no expression more pertinent to the Northern Ireland context than this formation – but what he said was that:

> '...there is a 'false self which develops on a compliance basis and is related in a passive way to the demands of external reality.' [66]

He went on to say:

> '...the false self becomes organised to keep the world at bay, and there is another true self hidden away and therefore protected.' [67]

I take this to mean that in an encounter with some external phenomena, the child, where it perceives a threat, or in meeting again a hurtful or damaging situation, can as a defence mechanism, create a 'false self' empowered to cope with this threat, thus protecting the 'true self'. This is a strategy we all develop in a variety of forms and to which we may be able to resort at various times, even as adults. Indeed, over time we may be able to use the device in creative ways to help us

---

[66] D.W. Winnicott (1988), *Human Nature,* Free Association Books, London

[67] D.W. Winnicott (1988) as cited

negotiate the stresses of everyday life. Now, it could be argued that Winnicott's ideas should be viewed as an aspect solely of infant and child development. We might rightly question why they should be of relevance to the adults in the workshop group and to the broader situation I apply it to more generally. To counter this line of argument I make the following points.

Throughout our development we make recourse to strategies we have learned in childhood. It is no great departure from the central tenets of psychoanalysis, or the therapeutic field more widely, to say that these carry over into later, adult experience. As we mature, we may or may not recognise them as they become incorporated into an adaptive repertoire of response and reaction. But, what happens *in extremis*? What goes on where a person is obliged to live in situations of great conflict? Could the impact of the kind of vigilance required in certain contexts of Northern Ireland produce a more virulent form of false self? Are there grounds to believe in the management of the often violent complexities of the political divide in Northern Ireland, that the individual carries on the notion of the false self into a full-blown adult version? If so, what is its purpose and what form might it take?

## The Survival Self

I suggest that in the context of the situation in Northern Ireland, where sectarian attitudes are universal that simply to maintain, many individuals develop a 'survival self'. This survival self is formed out of the same essential structures, the so-called 'defence organisation', that Winnicott discusses. It is a response that permits the individual to exist on an everyday basis, what Winnicott means by 'compliance', and could be a form of protection against the descent into a more compulsive and damaging paranoia. In survival self mode, the individual is prophylactically sheltering from the impact of the fear, trauma and dangers of the conflict situation. They exist in a kind of ennumbed state. In essence, some of the more sensitively attuned systems of the human encounter with the world are shut down. The individual, or the semblance of the person that is operative in the world at large, is active as a false, projected self, hiding the true self. Hence we see the case of the 'open and tolerant' persona emerging out of Northern Ireland, or the one which can cry at what happens there from the safe distance of the mainland, but can no longer weep *in situ*.

The psychic cost of maintaining the survival self is difficult to calculate or to overstate but one tentative estimation can be vouchsafed. To shut down those processes that are normally attuned to the enjoyment of the world must result in a loss of creative thrust and qualitative life. Winnicott talks of this vital imaginative interplay as happening in what he called a 'potential space'. It is crucial to the formation of ideas, vision and abstractions on how and why we exist. Sectarianism, and the response to it through the coping mechanism of the survival self, effectively shuts down this area. Winnicott explains the generalised symptomology of this maladaption in this lengthy but telling quote:

*'...It is probably wrong to think of creativity as something that can be destroyed utterly. But when one reads of individuals dominated at home, or spending their lives in concentration camps or under lifelong persecution because of a cruel political regime, one first feels that it is only a few of those victims who remain creative. These, are of course, the ones that suffer. It appears at first as if all the others who exist (not live) in such pathological communities have so far given up hope that they no longer suffer, and they have lost the characteristic that makes them human, so that they no longer see the world creatively. These circumstances concern the negative of civilization. This is looking at the destruction of creativity in individuals by environmental factors acting at a late date in personal growth.'* [68]

The import of such a construction for an organisation that has a primary focus on the play of children and a non-sectarian approach is worth some serious reflection.

If I might recite two anecdotes to enlarge this point. A baby is splashing with his mother in a swimming pool, two slightly older children join in with their playing, after a time they ask: "What is his name?" On being told, "Michael", they swim away. The child's name is sufficient to trigger the sectarian mechanism. Normally, the drive to play is so compelling that children will play when they are hungry, wet, or need to go to the lavatory – the image of a little boy hopping about clutching his willie but determined not to leave the game or whatever is something of a cliché. It is unusual to see a situation where the impulse to play is overlaid by a survival instinct. Such is the hold of the sectarian mind-set.

At the time of Drumcree, two children are in the back of a car, aggressively stopped by men of one tradition, with the marked effect that the children may be beginning the process that types them as being 'other' or apart. The mother who noted the reaction of her children to the men at the barricade may have registered the very point of formation of the survival self, constructed in membership of one form, that is putative tradition, by the rejection of another. That this is a happening to children in Northern Ireland is nothing short of a massive adulteration of the child's developing idea of the self as it should ideally be built up in the safe space of play.

It could be inferred from the idea of the false self and its evolution into an accepted part of a wider repertoire of response that it matures into a device that is healthy. This well-being is achieved, it would seem, by the 'playing out' of this material. The child can try on various guises and identities through play, testing the roles against 'real' situations in the safety of the play frame. It is out of this myriad of semblances that the personality gradually emerges. The sectarian construct intrudes into this frame and constricts the development offering only restricted forms of Identity. Sectarianism, deliberately shuts down play by suggesting that

---

[68] D.W. Winnicott (1992), *Playing and Reality,* Routledge, London

the imaginative creation of temporary identity is in fact a representation of the demonised other. The child can come to play only one game, sing one song, wear one colour. Among many other attributes sectarianism is a powerful method of internalised censorship.

Through such means the child is inducted into membership of one tradition or another. They learn to play the game (abide by the rules) of sectarianism. The child responds to this interference by accommodating it in the shape of the false self. Matters that also have a direct consequence for adults in the survival game of non-sectarianism. We, however, are obliged to recall that the individual has an identity that is constructed in play *before* the overlay of sectarian thinking, a 'true self, existing in an area that is *prior* to the adoption of behaviours that are sectarian. It is in the return to this original, true self, as adults, that our therapeutic endeavours should concentrate. This is not to break down immediately the survival self, the defence organisation is too well established to allow that. It is to recognise and understand It as a known pattern of response. At the very beginning of the workshop one member raised the idea that talking of sectarianism was a 'taboo'. Is it not rather that the taboo is in the breaching of the survival self, defence organisation? Does this not go some way to re-defining the nature of non-sectarian work?

## The Non-Sectarian Project

The project might be outlined in the following terms. If there is a direct link between the idea of the false self as it is attributed to the child and to a similar state in the adult, an interesting overlap accordingly emerges. It is precisely the area of the development of the false self and the continuance of this in adult form, in what I propose as the survival self, that a recognition and means of real non-sectarian working could take place. This elaboration has obvious implications for the workplace dedicated to such attitudes.

Accepting what I see as the pervasive nature of sectarianism in Northern Ireland, it is unlikely that an individual working in what might be described as a non-sectarian organisation could do so, and say, in all honesty, that they were themselves non-sectarian. What is more likely is there exist various degrees of co-option. This should simply be recognised. If this were made a more tacit disclosure then the organisation and the individuals concerned could set into place means by which this co-option could be countered. I contend that current non-sectarian work is in all probability being proposed as a cosmetic overlay. It exists in protocols and procedures but is really constructed as a means of tacit avoidance. (As a parallel example from the insights of the group, it has the same impact as the insistence, as an essential tenet of multi-culturalism in Northern Ireland, that playgroups should have Asian and black dolls!) I think it healthier that the likelihood of co-option, into drift or alignment with the traditions that dominate the scene, should be accepted and countered through the use of a re-aligning

64

deliberation. If I might, somewhat peremptorily take Playboard as a working example.

The first acknowledgement that is required is for individuals to recognise that they are sectarian as an inevitable consequence of their heritage. (Just as I am obliged to acknowledge my capacity for racism due to my heritage.) The next development is to seek to establish a means of recognising the invidious patterns of this behaviour, its contamination and co-options, and to counter them. This exploration must happen in safe space, I suggest this is a therapy space. It should be understood that no organisation in Northern Ireland can meaningfully deal with the issues of sectarianism unless such a space is established. In this space the workers can start to work on, to de-construct, the survival self. They could begin the process that will allow them to adapt this identity into new referential frameworks, developing an awareness of their internal, defence organisations and how they impact on their working practices.

Purely as an example, I would suggest that the team that underwent the two day workshop could use the same grouping as a co-counselling forum where they could work through the various problems they encounter in the field. Workers could exploit the group as a means of exorcising, prejudicial feelings, of overt identification with particular groups, or deep-seated, but, hitherto, unconscious, bias. It could also provide focus for sectors of practice where self-interest had led to some over-compensation. It is a space where we could reverse the normal polarity of professional functioning; here we could learn to be objective about ourselves and subjective about those we work with. It would have a high/risk high/trust constitution. I leave the crucial question of the support and facilitation of a group working in this way open for the moment.

All the parallels to play remain intact. The workers enter into a 'potential space' where they are permitted without censorship, hinder or let, to examine whatever they might feel about particular aspects of their work. They encounter again the creativity they can bring to bear in the tasks they undertake, the problems they must imaginatively solve. They can play out the encounters and fully explore the emotional impact of the task on their working lives. Co-workers, who might face each other from across a *defacto* divide of heritage and perception, can come to realise that under the skin, prior to the development of the limitations of the survival self, they have a shared commonality. One which pre-supposes, that before I am a member of a sect, I am human. This human commonality brings an authentic reality to non-sectarian work.

## To Conclude

As I write I am aware of a curious irony that has emerged. Those who are most caught up in sectarian myths may well be those who have the least well developed 'defence organisations'. Might this explain their allegiance and commitment to paramilitary factions *as a projected compensation*? They have abrogated their individuality into a collective, tribal identity of whatever cast. It is those who perceive this as damaging to their individuality who have retreated into the survival self. A position, therefore, which could be interpreted as the first step along the long road to psychological integration and to good mental health.

The rulings of the survival self Impose a 'technique of living' categorised by a definable loss of humanity. It is a reaction to the vicious imposition of what Foucault describes as 'the means of correct training'. From the perspective of the survival self we inflict the same regimes and the same rigours of 'correct' rejoinder on to our children and communities by repeating these patterns. If we can become aware of these patterns and begin the process of assimilating them into ever and ever richer repertoires of response we can offer a genuine form of self-healing, perhaps even to the body politic itself. Anthony Stevens, sets out just such a manifesto when he says:

> *'At the core of the shadow complex* [the Jungian idea of the other that carries those parts of ourselves we cannot accept] *is the archetype of the Enemy. Learning to live on good terms with 'the enemy within' means that one is less likely to project it on to other people, and, as a result, one makes one's minute contribution to peace and understanding in the world. What happens to the ego's relationship with the shadow is a transformation from the agonic to the hedonic mode: Instead of controlling (repressing) it or running away from it (denial), the ego initiates dialogue with the shadow, and, by confronting it and making efforts to befriend it, enters into a hedonic bond with it, thus rendering its energy available to the total personality.'* [69] (my definition in brackets)

I feel sure that the adoption of these ideas could make a major contribution to non-sectarian working practice. The trust, a crucial word, thus developed, could have a massive Impact on teambuilding, and coherent, practical, working objectives. Were such a hedonic method to be developed by any committed organisation, as a philosophical intent, it could underpin work across a huge range of activities, arenas and areas of conflict, beyond the confines of the Northern Ireland theatre.

## Gordon Sturrock
May 1997

---

[69] Anthony Stevens (1995), *Private Myths; Dreams and Dreaming,* Hamish Hamilton, London

# Constrained to be Free?
# – Aspirations and realities in playwork

Perry Else

## Prologue

I like to tell stories, usually to children, so if you'll bear with me for a while, I'd like to tell you about *The Little Prince*.[70]

The little prince was born on a small planet far way, with only a small rose and a couple of small volcanoes for company. He spent his time tending the rose and cleaning out the volcanoes until one day he set off on his adventures. He had lots of adventures on the planets between his home and Earth. He met a king who expects everyone to praise him, he met a conceited man who has no one to admire him and so expects the little prince to be in awe of him. He meets a business man who claims to own the stars — he has all the stars logged in his accountant book and he thinks these stars make him rich; so he spends all his time counting them to see how rich he his. The little prince meets many other foolish people before he comes to Earth but I do not have time today to tell you about them all.

While on this Earth, the little prince meets many things and sees roses far more beautiful than the weedy rose on his home planet. He also meets a wild fox.

The fox becomes entranced by the little prince and seeks to be tamed by him, to establish ties. And so over period of time the two become friends and the little prince tames the fox. The fox helps the little prince to see that the rose he cared for on his home planet was unique in all the world. The little prince sees that she is more important than all the hundreds of other roses he has seen.

> "Because it is she that I have watered; because it is she that I have sheltered behind the screen; because it is for her that I have killed the caterpillars (except the two or three that we saved to become butterflies); because it is she that I have listened to, when she grumbled, or boasted, or even sometimes when she said nothing. Because she is my rose."

And he went back to meet the fox. "Good-bye," he said.

"Good bye," said the fox. "And now here is my secret, a very simple secret: It is only with the heart that one can see rightly; what is essential is invisible to the eye."

"What is essential is invisible to the eye," the little prince repeated, so that he would be sure to remember.

---

[70] Antoine de Saint Exupéry (Reprint 1994), *The Little Prince*, Mammoth Books, London UK

"It is the time you have wasted for your rose that makes your rose so important."

"It is the time I have wasted for my rose—" said the little prince, so that he would be sure to remember.

"People have forgotten this truth," said the fox. "But you must not forget it. You become responsible, forever, for what you have tamed. You are responsible for your rose..."

"I am responsible for my rose," the little prince repeated so that he would be sure to remember.

## Introduction

I didn't know about *The Little Prince* when I started in playwork, though it was playwork that introduced me to him. If you would like to know more about him, then please read the book by Antoine de Saint Exupéry.

I've been asked today to let you know about the difficulties and possibilities that I see in play and playwork. I shall tell you a little about my own practice and relate that later to what I feel is missing from playwork practice.

## Possibilities and Aspirations

Like a lot of people in playwork, I got involved through adventure playgrounds. Way back then I didn't know about NVQs, though I did find out about LAPA/PLAYLINK. I was expected to 'do my best' which I've tried to do for most of the last fifteen years, but I hope I've also learned a little in that time. In the early days of my playwork practice, I discovered many of the possibilities that play and playwork hold for me today.

The first possibility was the space for children to learn to be themselves. Children came to this special space, the playground, to be something other than they were the rest of the day; it was the one place where they could do what they wanted to do – within limits that usually I set but with their collusion. Individuals came to play with groups, families came to play with friends, young carers came for respite, bullies came to be counselled. They learnt about life and death, love and hate, friendship and forgiveness.

I found that some children found the play experience to be therapeutic. Often they could not articulate their fears and terrors but a few hours on the playground helped them cope with it and go back to the real world a little refreshed. Occasionally children would open up to workers and we would find ourselves a little out of our depth in matters about which we were ill prepared. But we would help them the best way we could and usually it turned out for the best.

Next was the chance to be creative – children found that the rules on the playground were very friendly; they could dig, build dens, paint the shed, make a mural, play new games, act in a drama, be Michael Jackson for a day. Usually someone would have a radio or tape player and on sunny days impromptu discos would break out every so often.

Then came the chance to be tested, in the earliest days this was to test yourself against the terrors of the play equipment. As I worked closer with LAPA, this became more testing yourself against your own skills and abilities. Most children knew how to walk when they came to the playground, but a lot learnt how to climb, balance, jump and fall. For some there was also the challenge of dancing in public, talking in public, being applauded in public. For many this was their chance to experiment and test themselves in a 'safe' environment. Generally they felt comfortable with an audience of their peers and playworkers – who they generally saw as big kids anyway. It was this challenge that gave children the chance to develop themselves, they would stretch their bodies <u>and</u> their minds on the play ground.

For myself also, I had a feeling that this was important work. I discovered the possibility as a worker to reach a child profoundly and deeply, and it was this that has probably kept me in this work for so long – it's not been the pay! I never knew exactly what would reach a child, but I have been fortunate enough to have some feedback over the years, 'do you remember when...?' And of course I don't; I remember other occasions with that person, but obviously they weren't <u>the</u> key moments for them.

I also found that playwork was a great way of getting to meet the community. Sometimes it was parents coming down to complain, but usually it was people dropping in for a chat, or bringing a cup of tea. We'd get to find out what was going on around the playground and that would be useful in putting things into perspective all-round.

## Constraints and Realities

Because I was an eternal optimist in the early days, I learnt the constraints more slowly. And it has usually been later as a manager that my biggest lessons have been learned. These are not in any particular order, more that these are the ones that have stuck with me throughout my practice. So, the first one, playwork skill levels.

Using language from today, I like to think in my earliest days in playwork that I was *unconsciously competent*. Standards were different then, society was more tolerant and I did many things that wouldn't be permitted today. But I acted naturally with the children; was myself, played with them, was there when they wanted me, left them to themselves when I was dismissed. I then became *consciously incompetent*. I saw others in the play field who I respected and admired (some of them are here to day). I knew that I did not have all the skills and knowledge that they demonstrated and that I needed to be an effective playworker so set out to acquire them – I know I'm still looking.

I completed my National Playwork Accreditation Scheme portfolio in 1993 (at the second attempt) and so became *consciously competent*. As this was an early prototype for the NVQ, its currency has passed and I should now be seeking re-assessment. But my search for new skills has taken me in new directions and I will be leaving that one for the time being.

I must say that I found that whole process confidence building; while I held several formal qualifications, I was not a trained playworker and I felt a little bit of a fraud. The qualification validated what I had learned from my experience and so was very useful from that stand point. But it did not teach me anything about play. My knowledge about play I have developed over the years through much conscious reading, but I still feel that what I knew first has validity still. Speaking to some of our playworkers in Sheffield this summer, I confirmed this opinion. There were few good words to say about the NVQ. They found it 'all right' but it didn't teach them anything about play and on the whole they preferred a more traditional play qualification as it involved less paperwork and the pain was over with the examination.

Related to a lack of agreed skills, there continues to be a lack of clear standards for playwork. Perhaps I should rephrase that. Standards have come in like a sledgehammer over recent years and we now have the demands of the Children Act for play provision under eight, and safety concerns for every one else. But I'm talking here about a consistent approach to playwork and the value to be brought to our work. Our Play Policy for Sheffield has proved very useful as a way of setting agreed standards across the city. For example, the development of a 'kite-mark' for early years provision that is being led by our Young Children's Service. This kite-mark is being developed jointly by play and care providers in the statutory and voluntary sectors through a series of 'study groups' where self evaluation is helping set a clear standard for all. Of course within this there has to be a clear value base that allows for dialogue and debate so that all are learning – rather than simply agreeing with the more forceful members of the group. We are also drawing up a clear playground strategy that puts play value ahead of other criteria such as ease of maintenance and access to the supplier.

And of course I have found that resources have had a profound effect on the quality and standard of play provision. Fifteen years ago we complained about not having enough but without exception things have got tighter every year. For example, over ten years ago in Sheffield there was a thriving adventure playground association with over ten active members. There are now two playgrounds and both are ran by the city council. Our grants budget has been cut every year, despite rhetoric about the value of children's work – we have been a victim of the reducing levels of resource to local authorities like Sheffield and the large capital projects that the department built in 1991.

Rather than say that there is not enough money available for play (there is not enough available for <u>everything</u>), we now say that not enough is prioritised for play. We have had to learn how to argue the value of play provision through other measures such as value for money when contrasted with the youth service, or from a community safety perspective where we aim to divert young people from crime. Both of these positions do not recognise play as play for its own sake, but we have had to go beyond trying to argue this position. We live in a hard economic world where most people know the price of everything and the value of nothing.

Chief amongst the difficulties, I have found that the lack of a shared, clear theoretical base has affected playwork – put ten playworkers together in a room and you will usually have eight different theories of play and two anarchists. This leads to workers making 'professional judgements from a spurious, personal background, and which I believe feeds the over-reliance on wanting to make play provision 'safe', an impossible goal.

In extending my own play theory, I have come across the work of Gerald Edelman, who argues from the biological, physiological perspective. Edelman is beginning to show that the brain learns through a process of 'natural selection'.

An example of this is when a baby starts grasping for an object. A computer would receive a programme that said something like; 'raise arm, extend for 30 cm at 90º, close hand, contract to starting position (or mouth, ear, whatever)'. Babies don't learn like this, they spend ages trying to understand that the object out there is a separate identity, then even longer trying to get their arm to go in the right direction. And when it's in the right direction they need to learn how to grasp. It is by 'playing' with all the possibilities that they eventually come up with the right combination, but then lose it again! By constant practice it then becomes second nature and in that they learn that a similar process can be used to grasp anything that is out there. In the process they learn about gravity, velocity, simple geometry, dimension and themselves.

The brain (and so the child) needs diversity, interaction and choice – the chance to play – if it is to develop; it is not a computer waiting for an instruction from an external programmer:

> 'For Edelman, the brain is a generator of new behaviour. It reacts to the world in a totally unique way, motivated by its own system of values. If you substitute the word 'person' for the word 'brain', that statement is a summary of the idea of individual freedom of action. For Edelman, we are our brains, and because of this, we must construct our own version of the world. We are, in a sense, constrained to be free.' [71]

This tells me, that the free choice and focus of play is literally the chance to develop into a functioning, balanced adult. A child denied this opportunity will become stuck at some stage of their personal development, be it their confidence in using their body to its utmost or

---

[71] David Sington et al (1994), *The man who made up his mind*, BBC, London UK

the development of themselves, their mature ego. I now strongly believe that the role of playworkers is to help children past these blocks, to take them back to a place where they feel comfortable and able to take risks again so that they can choose to relive or play through an experience and learn from it in a safe environment.

## A Unified Theory of Play?

In summary I feel that the major difficulties in playwork today are caused by a lack of understanding about the nature and function of play; all those working in play being able to clearly answer the question, 'what is play' at a deeper level than 'SPICE' allows. This knowledge would impact on the importance of play as seen by those who control play provision or have an influence in how it is delivered.

I feel that a 'unified theory of play' is what is missing from our playwork practice. A theory that all work within would help our profession move forward with the respect it should command. This ability to describe clearly the nature of play and its importance in human development would end the vagueness around the value of play. When playworkers are seen as people to be valued for the skills and insight they can bring to a child's development, our status and standing will change dramatically.

This is a challenge, for we have already begun to define and describe the play behaviours we see in playwork – we have even tried to describe the 'underpinning knowledge' – all these things are in the NVQ units and elements. What we have not yet described is the mystery of play, that which the 'heart sees rightly; (that which) is essential is invisible to the eye.' I'm confident that before very much longer, we will be able to read about a 'unified theory' that all (except perhaps the anarchists) can support.

Until then I feel we need to work within the constraints imposed on us by circumstance and authority – we need to find a way to be free enough to do our work good enough. The challenge is ours; children don't demand this but they do need it.

In the meantime we battle away trying to hold our corner. In Sheffield our Play Policy has been a vital part in promoting the value and importance of play provision.

Since the adoption of the policy last year, the Policy has led to many things including:

- Article 31 of the United Nations Convention on the Rights of the Child being adopted by the Council

- An audit of expenditure, especially around fixed play equipment being commissioned

- An additional £35,000 of summer playscheme funds being targeted at disadvantaged communities

- A joint Lottery Bid for the establishment of Play Council, a partnership body to promote play
- Promotion of the value of play across many council departments and with councillors
- Joint play provision supported by Housing and Social Services departments
- Work with schools and nurseries on raising the quality of the outdoor environment

In Sheffield we see the need to be practical, to get the job done within the current difficulties of the work, but we still like to look to the stars to inspire us.

## End-piece

I'd like to finish with another extract from *The Little Prince*.

In another part of his story, he meets a railway switchman who's job it is to sort out travellers sending them off one way and another. The little prince notices that everyone is in a hurry looking for something and no one seems to be satisfied with where they are. The switchman describes the travellers;

> "They are asleep in there, or if they are not asleep they are yawning. Only the children are flattening their noses against the window panes."

> "Only the children know what they are looking for," said the little prince. "They waste their time over a rag doll and it becomes very important to them; and if anybody takes it away from them, they cry..."

> "They are lucky," said the switchman.

Until everyone has their nose at the window, we need to be advocates on behalf of children and play – finding ways round the constraints so that we and all the children we work with can be free to play.

**Perry Else**
November 1997

# 'The Colorado Paper' - The Playground as Therapeutic Space: Playwork as Healing

## Gordon Sturrock and Perry Else

> *'Chinese baseball is played almost exactly like American baseball – the same field, players, bats and balls, method of scoring, and so on. The batter stands in the batter's box, as usual. He winds up, as usual, and zips the ball down the alley. There is only one difference, and that is: After the ball leaves the pitcher's hand, and as long as the ball is in the air, anyone can move any of the bases anywhere.'* [72]

Fred Donaldson

Throughout this paper, we use the term playworker to describe adults active in play work with children. Of course, this description is intended to include parents and other adults active in playing with children.

Similarly, we use the term child or children interchangeably, as a playworker may work with one child or with several. We also use the plural term 'they' alongside the single term 'child' in preference to the more traditional male form 'his' or the currently used 'he/she' or 'his/hers'.

In common with the long established academic practice of the lead author taking precedence in co-written papers, this edition correctly places Gordon Sturrock ahead of Perry Else. The original alphabetical citation was due to an administrative error at the time of the IPA/USA 1998 Conference and is happily corrected with this edition of **'The Colorado Paper'**.

## Preamble

> *'The subject matter …is not that collection of solid, static objects extended in space but the life that is lived in the scene that it composes; and so reality is not that external scene but the life that is lived in it. Reality is things as they are.'* [73]

If not yet exactly established as a profession there is a job widely described as playworker; that is, a person who works with children in the expansion of their potential to explore and experience through play. Out of a curious hotchpotch of philosophies, writings and findings there has existed – if not exactly thrived – this separate and particular discipline in the United Kingdom. Behind it is a movement which concludes that play has great importance for the development of the young child. Until the more recent and increasingly compelling appetite to have play incorporated into care situations, this movement centred

---

[72] Fred Donaldson (1993), *Playing by Heart*, HCI. Publications, Deerfield Beach, Fla. USA

[73] Stanislav Grof (1993), *The Holotropic Mind*, Harper Collins, New York, USA

around the choices of the child for content and containment. Provision was focused on the child's desire or drive to play. The central ethos was that the children themselves made the decisions about what and where they played and for how long. The adults who staffed these centres acted as resources for this self-directed play.

The perspective that we outline in this paper is arrived at from this particular working context; that is, playwork as it is understood in the UK within, particularly, adventure playgrounds, as secure, boundaried spaces where children choose and order their own playing. Here, the job of the playworker might be described, to be brief, as 'freely associating in the free association of children.'

We suggest, that in an environment where the natural space for play (both physical and psychic) is steadily being eroded, where the playful habitat – or more widely what we describe as the *ludic ecology* – is being curtailed or contaminated, we see increasing signs of breakdown and dis-ease. In response, playsites are coming to serve as 'authorised' grounds for children's play. Here, the work of the adult in playgrounds is required to fulfil a more curative function than has hitherto been acknowledged. It is from this new viewpoint that we suggest that playspace should now be seen as *therapeutic space* and playwork advanced as having an unexplored, healing potential.

## Introduction

*'There are two ways of doing injury to mankind: one, the introduction of pains; the other, exclusion of pleasures. Both are acts of tyranny, for in what does tyranny consist, if not in this?'* [74]

Jeremy Bentham

In our opinion, the position of playwork in the United Kingdom at present is fraught. Playwork has failed to flourish for the following reasons:

- our inability to constitute the functions of playwork as a widely accepted discipline

- our failure to carry off any kind of successful campaign or political lobby

- the rise of playcare as a solution to the social problem of the working parent and the resulting impact on slender resources for play

- and the inability of the field itself to take on and advance the movement through meaningful research and development.

The idea of adventure play is under serious challenge, and with it all that the open accessibility ethos meant to our ideas on play. What was

---

[74] Jeremy Bentham, *Theory of Legislation*, quoted in Rebecca Abramos (1997), *The Playful Self*, Fourth Estate, London UK

a widespread and (at least in London) an organisationally cohesive entity, has become disparate and fragmented. Adventure play – and its ideals, they merit such a description – has come to be seen as a discipline that is out of place and out of tune.

Work in play is increasingly presented in the forms emerging out of playcare practice and is based on early year's education. As the ideological basis of playcare is often constructed in the arguments of adult convenience, rather than in the child's essential developmental processes, this has meant a considerable shift in practice. The underpinning philosophical thesis for this shift is conveniently ignored.

However, playwork has been unable to offer an alternative to playcare's justification in terms of social need. This is because playwork has little or no convincing theoretical base to argue its own case for developmental contribution. Social pressures have allowed for it to be easily co-opted into the growing domain of playcare, resulting in playwork provision and especially open access practice steadily being diminished.

The outcome for playwork has been a retreat into more concrete forms of work and the need to identify with some other profession for comfort. A number of playworkers have come to consider 'professional' status as being a cover for the field's lack of authority and esteem. Ideas of play, in the current view, are best couched safely in terms of other, more respected professions (the teacher, the social worker and so on), not out of our own experience. Playwork has drifted into a kind of inauthentic voice; this may account for the difficulty of translating 'what we know into what we say'. In contrast to this, we must note a certain maturity in the discipline itself seeking to establish real purpose and meaning for play work. However these comments are whispered asides compared to the loud voices of the 'play programme' and 'practical frameworks' active in the field.

Broadly speaking, in playwork, there appear to be two schools of thought: those who see the practice as having worth solely in soft forms of social control (what Foucault termed 'the means of correct training'), and those who wish to move deeper into comprehending what our contact with children at play might mean. That is, a recognition of play as having a *child-ordinated, healing potentiality* with which we work. It is this notion, that we attempt here to explain and develop, and which, we argue, should more fittingly form playwork's manifesto.

## The Application

*'Beyond its role in emotional regulation, self-soothing, arousal, and formation of neurosis and even character, fantasy can act as a rehearsal for future action and can provide a template for life choices that may be either literal translations (enactments) or symbolic*

*expressions of the fantasy's narrative content. Fantasy is a theatre in which we preview the possible scenarios of our life to come.'* [75]

Many with whom we have discussed the content of this paper and its underlying propositions have seen the introduction of therapeutic ideas into the playwork approach as at odds with one of its stated aims, that is, child ordinated activity. We refute this. Much of the application discussed here is based directly, on and out of, our working practices as long-time playworkers, managers and policy makers. What we suggest here is not a departure from the first principles of playwork but rather a return to them. We simply point to a more transcendent means of working, and as an inevitable consequence, playwork is described in new forms with a new vocabulary. We contend, however, that we are merely articulating what many playworkers have felt to be the essential exchanges of their work. We have only attempted to state these in more precise terms.

Everyone working in play may have to face the fact that the idea of playwork is undergoing change. We argue that there exists the potential for it to degenerate into types of 'soft policing'. Although couched in terms of a return to the original ideas of play and playwork, what we go on to outline needs to be understood in a more radical and diagnostic form. We regard this as a more reflective, contemplative, kind of working. We offer the following 'explanation sketch' as the first provisional explication of the idea of a more therapeutic approach to playspaces, and to playwork practice, with an emphasis on its ameliorating or healing potential.

Accordingly, we have placed the movement and actions of play into a more systematic application. In this structure, the various forms (or matrices) serve the function of amplifying the content of the play exchange, setting, or artefact, better to explore its deeper meaning, within a series of levels helping judgement and interpretation. This entire construct, and the overall approach that emerges, views play practice from a more interpretative and analytic perspective. A generalised proposition that might more properly be termed *psycholudics*, the study of the mind or psyche at play.

Essentially, each identification or construct functions as an initiating 'stepping off point' into a more symbolic understanding of play. This is an understanding that the playworker is required themselves to elaborate in their practice. Our thesis rests on one essential proposition; that before and prior to each act of creativity of the child lies an imaginal realm or zone that is playful (*ludic*) and symbolically constituted. The playworker joins and works with this zone of *emergent material* and content. The practice is not a reductive response to the play acts and settings observed; it is not trying to control or manage the material or action. It does rest in the richness of response or 'ecstasy of variety' that a play exchange, setting or artefact generates.

---

[75] Ethel S Person (1996), *The Force of Fantasy*, Harper Collins, London, UK

This is the proper measurement of the inherent play values of our methods and work.

The consequence of all this, is that in the play encounter, the drive active in the play setting (or stage, frame, playground, in the toy, artefact, game, ritual, rite) is contained and reflects, or is reflected back, to the child or player. This containment and the resulting boundary (or frame) 'holds' the meaning or intentionality of the child's play; that is, the environment or the worker gives some answer to the question the child has issued. This space is, in essence, the platform for the symbolic forms of 'stadial' development that the child is expressing, and which we, as playworkers, may be asked to acknowledge *with*, and on occasion, *for* them. Out of this material, it is possible for the playworker to develop insights and interpretative responses aiding further, and perhaps deepening, expression of this *ludic content*. When recognition of this issue and response fails, when the cycle becomes hybrid, when the containment breaks or ruptures, we get forms of *dysplay* – driven play material will out anyhow – taking over.

Is the hybrid maladapted play cycle, the kernel of neurosis? If almost all psychologies of depth, or therapies, are the archaeology, or the 're-playing' of neurosis formed in childhood, we might argue that the playworker is active at the *precise point* where potential neuroses are being formed. We therefore ask the following questions: might playworkers enable the 'playing out' of actual neurotic formation as a basic element of our practice? Could playwork be seen as being curative? Our responses to these questions form the core of this paper.

## The Setting

*'When otherness is disavowed by the psyche, we are truly in the Theatre of the Impossible, but since the play cannot go on stage without the complicity and credence of others who are not mere inventions of the subject's imagination (even if they are treated as such), the whole performance is also under the sway of external reality and thus is subject to the limitations of the Possible.'* [76]

The setting or background we discuss is largely that of the playworker who is active – that is, themselves *freely associating, in the free associations of children*. This form of play is most redolent of the principles of playwork as practised in adventure playgrounds in the United Kingdom (though there are numerous other applications that we will not explore in this paper). This having been accepted, we propose that in the various containments of the playground and particularly, the more intimate and subtle 'frames' of their play and games, children will produce or engage with the same material generated in the frame of analysis or therapy. By this we mean unconscious imagery, motifs and symbolic substance. This we see as the fundamental working material of a therapeutic playwork practice.

---

[76] Joyce McDougall (1986), *Theatres of the Mind*, Free Association Books, London. UK

Playworkers are, in effect, engaging with both (i), an obvious and manifest level of playing and (ii), a deeper more latent layer of unconscious, but now emerging, content. This, in essence, suggests that the playworker is active in the same potent area of psychodynamic effects as therapists or analysts. Indeed we go further. We suggest that the playworker may well be immersed (and for greater periods of duration and time) in the very medium that therapists and analysts exploit in their therapeutic endeavours without accounting for this in terms of our practice. In playwork, we are in contact with material to do with the emotional and affective expression of the child's life-world and identity. But, in current descriptions of our work as in the 'coming-to-consciousness' expression of the playing child, we ourselves are, at least with regard to our practice, operating unconsciously.

We can think of no greater barrier to the deepening of our work than this unexplored dimension. The concepts we go on to discuss go some way to addressing this lack. To this end, we have examined the fields of the depth psychologies for some of the material we discuss here. In general, we are in accord with Adler when he said:

> 'The manner in which a child approaches a game, his choice and the importance he places on it, indicate his attitude and relationship to his environment and how he's related to his fellow man.' [77]

## Some Conceptual Considerations on Play and the Ludic

> 'All of these theories seem to have some validity, but we are still awaiting an elegant, unifying 'grand' theory, of play that integrates all its positive qualities.' [78]

It is a commonplace in various texts on the subject to read that play has some essence that is hard to define, some ineffable quality. The encounter with the phenomena of play appears to shape a desire to explore indescribable *qualia*, inspiring both heartfelt eulogy and massive evasion from playworkers. Somehow, humankind's drive to play – the Sanskrit idea of *lila* captures this most closely, play as divine; seen in the urge to invent, to create – is set aside for more routine or mundane matters.

For the first part, this evasion can be seen in the denial of this desire, or this drive, as being an attendant part of our existential idea of maturation. In short, that we have come to operate in a 'conceptual straight-jacket' in understanding play and its role and function in human development. In an urge to educate our children to face a future we can only fearfully intuit, we adulterate an area that the authors choose to describe as a *ludic ecology*. It is this ludic habitat, at the most

---

[77] Alfred Adler (1994), as quoted in *The Quotable Play Therapist*, Jason Aronson Inc, Northvale, NJ. USA

[78] Charles Schaefer (1993), *The Therapeutic Powers of Play*, Jason Aronson Inc, Northvale, NJ. USA

internalised of levels, that we are unwittingly polluting. The cost may be seen in our inability to recognise the transcendent possibilities of playwork.

Stanislav Grof reminds us that:

> 'Inner transformation can be achieved only through individual determination, focused effort, and personal responsibility. Any plans to change the situation in the world are of problematic value, unless they include a systematic effort to change the human condition that has created the crisis. To the extent to which evolutionary change in consciousness is a vital prerequisite for the future of the world, the outcome of this process depends on the initiative of each of us.' [79]

By means of this paper, we attempt to outline an idea of play and the ludic within a new paradigm. We suggest that the purpose of play is precisely in what might be termed a *consciousness*, seen, as Pierce has it, as the 'behaviour of behaviours.' Or as an awareness that is the prefiguring (but always present) element of all creativity. We propose that this ground consciousness is the source of all mental health and well being and that it should be viewed as a particular, *ludic ecology*. In this place lies a means of healing trauma, neurosis and psychic ill through play.

The playwork schema that follows rests on an understanding of play as being a drive active in a *frame* of a particular nature. This frame is the stage or setting that offers the important containment and return for the child's *issued driven material, cues and themes*. In this frame, the play drive seeks and requires accommodation, both physical and non-physical, and reflection, in the sense of a mirroring back – a *return* as we put it – to be enacted. It suggests that some elements of the play setting or playground's function will be compensatory for, and contributory to, the emotional equilibrium of the child. It further suggests that at the deeper levels of functioning, the child will be expressing, in symbolic form, unconscious material crucial to their psychic development that will also require containment, reflection and return and thoughtful engagement by the involved playworker.

In this compact, the task of the playworker may be to consider and develop an interpretative or analytic perspective out of which to issue their responses. From this pattern of issue and return the playworker can provide some counterpoise in the constituent life-world of the child. It is the consistent operation of this response that most clearly marks the work of the playworker. The constructs we go on to explicate attempt to place this reflective response into a framework as an aid to the playworker active in this delicate area of operation.

---

[79] Stanislav Grof (1985), *Beyond the Brain*, State University of New York, New York, USA

## Some Definitional Background

*'The aspect of things that are most important for us are hidden because of their simplicity and familiarity.'* [80]

Ludwig Wittgenstein

As an aid to understanding, we suggest a series of propositions that underpin our approach to playwork. In this application, the practice is seen from a deeper more interpretative, perhaps analytical perspective. We concentrate on the more tactical and technical aspects of the interchanges of play, *the interplay phenomena*, those that happen within the interpersonal, emotional affects of the work, rather than evaluations of the more physical or concrete elements of the site, setting and practice. (These are already well considered, and we would refer interested parties to the many publications that have covered this important aspect of the task. For example, see Hughes, A Question of Quality, 1996, and others.)

What follows here is not to do with those manifest elements of play work but with what we see as its more latent and underlying phenomena; the aspects of the *ludic*, its non-physical or psychic dimensions, rather than the physical aspects of play practice. To begin.

## The Play Process

The cyclic processes of play are often referred to but have not been set into a coherent formulation; the most common descriptions adhere to simple explanations of cycles of creation and destruction. These need to be considerably enlarged. We propose the following formula as being a more accurate rendition of the looping cycle of play, seen and understood as a drive. For our purposes, the play process has four, key, functional components.

These are:

**M-L:** the meta-lude; from which the drive or cue to play is issued to the environment.

**T>:** the termination or decay; the breakdown of this drive over time.

**@:** the active development; the response to the play cue by the environment or another player.

**§:** the loop and flow; the response is picked up, processed and acted on in the metaludic space.

The resulting formula expresses the ludic cycle (**L**) – thus:

**L = (M-L. T>. @. §)**, where if **@** or **§** are absent the cycle ends.

---

[80] Ludwig Wittgenstein (1995), as quoted in *Zen Diary*, Workman Publishing, NY, USA

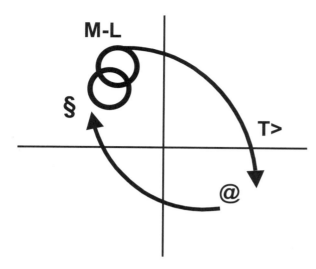

The essential task of the playworker is to be in service of this process as it unfolds **M-L**, decays **T>**, or is developed **@** in the playing child. Playwork actions and interventions can be understood and perfected around an essential understanding of the various phases of this *ludic cycle* with appropriate readings and responses being established. To steal a march on a later and fuller explanation, the playworker must 'co-operate intelligently' with the cyclic, playing processes of the child or children.

## The Play Drive or Ludido
*(after Sturrock 1993, and Sturrock and Rennie 1995/97)*

> 'The chimpanzee used the stone much as a child uses the transitional object. This... suggests that primates other than humans engage in some forms of symbolic play. Taken together with other disparate pieces of evidence, ...we might infer that we are born with a propensity, instinct, or drive to play.'[81]

This derivation sees the play function as a basic biological drive. We know that all mammals and many animals play. Play therefore is more than simply a behaviour; rather there is a deeper motivation serving biological and existential purposes. The driven energy of play is not just expended or spent, it is effectively an issue and response, ludic, feedback loop. For our means, the essential cycle can be discerned in the cues that the child issues to the surrounding environment, objects and others and the returning material that they compose in the play frame. It is more than a mere rehearsal for adulthood – this is to diminish and adulterate its purpose – it is instead a series of playful investigations that form the life-world of the child and their sense of identity and self. Russell Meares writes:

> 'The pole of consciousness that James called the I, moved the contents of consciousness about in an associative or combinatory play. A very important implication of this description is that consciousness is not merely passive, a simple searchlight, but active.'[82]

---

[81] Russell Meares (1993), *The Metaphor of Play*, Jason Aronson Inc, Northvale, NJ, USA

[82] Russell Meares (1993), as cited

We suggest, as a distinct playwork definition, that the *ludido*, the play drive, could be precisely seen as the active agency of an evolving consciousness – such a description is closer to the definitions out of eastern psychologies and traditions, the lila principle – in what we call a 'field' or psychic, ludic ecology.

## Metalude

We see this formulation as one of the most intangible but important areas of the working practice of the playing children and the adult/practitioner active in that play. As it is crucial to what follows we provide a lengthy description of its relevance and validity to our task. We draw on much of the work of Winnicott and a number of other analysts and therapists for the essential construction of our thesis, but feel it important to state that the reference point, for the main part, is out of our direct experience of playwork practice. Winnicott himself provides the justification. He said:

> '*I am reaching towards a new statement of playing, and it interests me when I seem to see in the psychoanalytic literature the lack of a useful statement on the subject of play. Child analysis of whatever school is built around the child's playing, and it would be rather strange if we were to find that in order to get a good statement about playing we have to go to those who have written on the subject who are not analysts.*'[83]

We take up the challenge. A part of the play drive or ludido is sustained in a deeply internalised form of fantasy play, which we observed from our play practice, and that we have confirmed out of our work in play practice and in therapies. This internalised zone is variously described, most notably by Winnicott, who called it the 'third area' and 'the potential space'. He invested it principally with qualities from his psychoanalytic, object relations, perspective.

To differentiate and to acknowledge some of the functionality ascribed from out of eastern psychological practices, where play, or *lila*, could be seen as being 'the divine diversion or play of appearances dreamed up by the gods for their amusement' – we might be talking of the gods appearing in the frame of the child's play – we describe it as a distinct and operative zone profoundly relevant to our working method. One of the authors of this paper saw this *metalude* as a higher form of play. It is the source point and beginning of the function of *internalised gestalt formation* within the play process already outlined.

Children at play engage in the production and sharing of *internalised gestalts*; they are 'alive in the moment', with no concern for the past or future. Playworkers discern these gestalts through experiential insight; they *feel* them, even if the external, physical evidence is slight. The encounter of the child and the adult in any play setting involves, in part,

---

[83] D.W. Winnicott (1992), *Playing and Reality*, Routledge, London and New York

an overlapping of this gestalted material. In some cases, the child's and the playworker's effects become merged to form a new intrasubjective identity; a ludic third, or a *gestalted mutuality*. This is when people play together and 'get lost' in their play. These formations first appear in what we call the *metaludic* space of play. (This can also be the case with a group where there would be a collective, overlapping mutuality, the point being that the 'getting lost' is expanded to the group.) Playwork practice may require an involvement sensitised to contact with this subtle emerging material and its issuing centre.

Recent developments in psychoanalytic discourse suggest this 'centre' as being the source of all curative, therapeutic outcomes. A cure or healing, that therapists steadfastly maintain is constituted in their own interpretative practice, Freudian, Kleinian, or whatever. We suggest that it is act of playing that has the healing inherent in it. A point to which we will return later.

## The Ludic Ecology

Current descriptions of the life-world and development of identity and self – the Heideggerian notion of *dasein*, self-being, has some relevance – have not been fully appreciated by the playwork discipline. Neither have they begun, as yet, to influence our disciplinary discourse. We offer the construction of the psychic, ludic ecology as a first tentative translation of some of these ideas into our practice. Meares points out the nature of this locus:

> '*The play of the very young child has peculiar characteristics that include the relationship with the other, the form of language, and an absorption in the activity that is similar to that of an adult who is lost in thought. The field of play is where, to a large extent, a sense of self is generated.*' [84]

This *field* is the ethereal stage, the play frame, the potential space, that incorporates *internal* symbolic representations and *external* artefacts, objects and others; these serve to mirror and reflect the internalised drama or narrative. This stage can be seen as the psychic dimension of the child's playing eco-system. The resulting formation is in a direct and communicating relationship with their environmental surroundings. It is at the precise point of this encounter, the internalised play space of the child and its meeting with the external world, that the playworker sits poised. It is the 'field' of this internalised play, its throw or overlap with that of other children and that of the attendant playworker, in concert with the reflective, containment of the artefact, object, play frame and site, that composes the *ludic ecology*. This is not a solid formation, it is rather a fluid and supple projection. The developing child's playful sense of self and identity is neither yet fixed nor bound by the soma or body form. Identity (and its lack!) does not end at the skin. Rather it is a

---

[84] Russell Meares (1993), as cited

mobile, flexible extension, where options, ideas, themes, change and adapt in contact with the surrounding, and containing, environment.

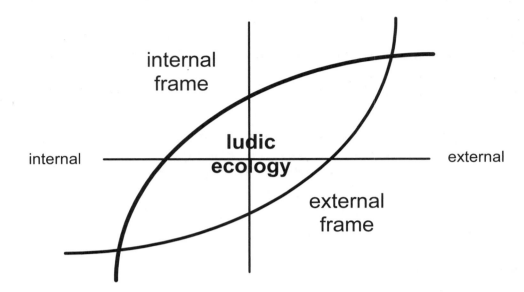

Much can be interpreted from the child's exploitation of external play objects, in conjunction with themes, magic or mythic material, and narrative constructs coming out of this delicate internal zone. This interplay we propose should be seen as a *ludic consciousness*, Edith Cobb, describes it thus:

> *'The child's urge to 'body forth the forms of things unknown' in the microcosm of child art and play bears a distinct resemblance to the morphogenesis characteristic of nature's long-term history, namely, evolution.'* [85]

To further extend the metaphor, we might perceive the child's play universe and the meeting with the external world as a flexible, holistic and ludic process. This totality we see as being a psychic, non-physical, ludic ecology. By 'reading' the inherent encounter and the subsequent balancing, the resulting adaption and adjustment processes, we as playworkers can contribute to the child's development in a way that is child-centred, and encourage the self-healing potentials of play to take effect.

## The Play Frame

Within the generalised summaries of playwork, there are well considered and articulated descriptions of some of the play frames that the child encounters. These have tended to be concerned with the physical aspects of the playground and play setting. There are, however, any numbers of subtle overlapping frames occurring simultaneously, to which the playworker must be sensitive. These frames are not physical but are projected or 'thrown' fantasy.

---

[85] Edith Cobb (1994), from *The Quotable Play Therapist*, Jason Aronson Inc, Northvale, NJ, USA

They can extend from the tiniest and most intimate, encompassing the child in some internalised reverie, lost in thought, daydreaming, to groups of children ranging across the wide open spaces of some of our larger playgrounds, where the entire space is the frame of the play. There will also be some overlap in terms of content, different groupings made up of players, happening across themes, games, narratives and so on, to fantasy constructs shared by small groups where the play is effectively virtual. The duration of these frames can be literally seconds to many weeks, even months. The frame will last as long as it has relevance and meaning for the projected play form of the child.

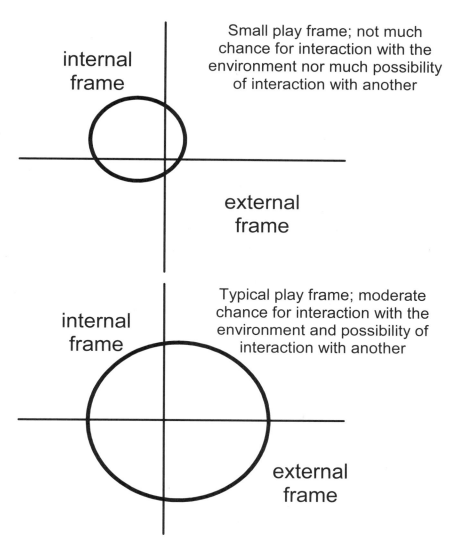

internal frame

Small play frame; not much chance for interaction with the environment nor much possibility of interaction with another

external frame

internal frame

Typical play frame; moderate chance for interaction with the environment and possibility of interaction with another

external frame

The most important function of the frame is that it provides the context or stage where the play form is enacted. The *play frame* is the holding limitation or boundary for the projected ludic material of the child's play. It is, in effect, the enclosure for their imaginal expression. It is chosen and initiated by the child and is a retainer for meaning and is a reflective vehicle for this meaning. It has a functional requirement to provide return. The play frame becomes ineffective, ruptured or decayed, when it can no longer offer this return. Arnold Modell, describes this contradictory necessity, thus:

> *'Ritualised rules of the game demarcate or frame a reality that is separated from that of ordinary life. This not something that Winnicott wrote about; but his theory of playing illustrates a profound paradoxical truth: That the freedom of play – that is, the freedom to create – exists only by means of constraint.'* [86] (our emphasis)

The play frame could therefore be viewed as a child initiated, non-material, constraint or boundary that helps define and give meaning to play content.

## Containment

> *'Heidegger explicitly rejects the idea of freedom as 'a free floating arbitrariness', insisting that we can understand 'freedom in its finitude' only if we see that 'proving boundedness' does not impair freedom.'* [87]

As a necessary distinction, the frame is the play boundary of the child. *Containment* is the 'holding' function of the playworker. If the play frame is the narrative thread, the theme, activity or game, that the child uses to bound their idea or notion of play, the playworker's responsive task is the crucial provision of containment. Again, this has largely been understood as being referenced to the purely physical aspects of the work, the site as a container, and has been taken to an extreme in playcare with content and programme provided by the adult. Our proposition is a greatly enlarged idea akin to Winnicott's notion of the 'holding' environment.

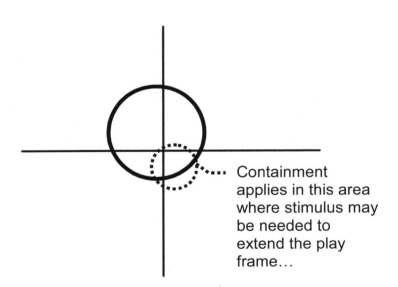

Containment applies in this area where stimulus may be needed to extend the play frame...

---

[86] Arnold Modell (1990), Tactics and Techniques in Psychoanalytic Therapy, vol. III, Jason Aronson Inc, Northvale, NJ, USA

[87] Charles Guignon (1993), Heidegger: A Critical Reader, Blackwell Publishers, Cambridge Mass., USA and Oxford, UK

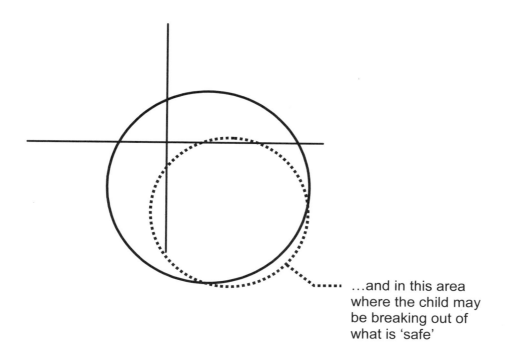

...and in this area
where the child may
be breaking out of
what is 'safe'

This is not the place to examine this idea fully, but, from observations of our own playwork experiences and those of others, we suggest that the play drive will, from time to time, need a holding or containing environment. This is particularly necessary during specific phases in the ludic loop of playing, most crucially to prevent a descent into the de-constructive, destructive phase of playing, or at its completed annihilation; that is, when the play value of a frame or theme is spent. (As a further aside, we also suggest that Winnicott's idea of the 'transitional object' has wider implications than simply as a descriptive dimension of solely an infant's behaviour. It may be that there is a process of 'transitional objectifying' that could be seen as the trigger or signal, a play cue, of such a breach occurring, a reaching out of the established frame. In adult or mature areas of life, this may signify movements of transition or transcendence to higher states of consciousness. The rehearsal quality of play may be the developing acceptance of the termination of well-used but redundant concepts.)

In containment, the playworker maintains the reflective integrity of the 'play frame' of the child. The task is in *recognising and preserving* the meaning of the play *at that time*. At some point, containment may alter when the attendant playworker, 'reading' the playful exchanges of the child, will enter the interrupted, decayed, disrupted cycle of play, and 'hold' or 're-frame' the play form with the children. Obviously, this is a delicate and sensitive task and open to many kinds of adulteration, but it is one we see as being central to the judgement and skills of playwork practice.

For example, it might most clearly be the case when the play frame has been prematurely terminated by external cessation, where play begins to reform into rules, where the play may need some ritual or rite, or celebratory elaboration to 'fix' the meaning. It is precisely a 'boundedness' that is 'proved' by the playing child's 'freedom' to use and discard it momentarily, without the playworker being discomfited by this apparent paradox.

The ludic feedback cycle has a natural form of decay, that is the child tires of that form, has derived whatever they need from it and it is deconstructed and replaced by new forms. There is also an unnatural form where the play is terminated or interrupted by external events or circumstances. Seen in this latter context, one of the playworker's tasks may be to provide the means of containing the meaning of the child's play as the frame is re-formed, is re-constructed or re-framed. In effect, the playworker becomes *the holder of meaning* for the child for periods of time. If containment is neglected, or is set aside for the playworker's needs or their own unplayed out material, the play is contaminated or adulterated.

## Play Cues
*(after Rennie and Sturrock [88])*

Observations of the child at play from the very earliest days of life show that they issue series of subtle cues to the surrounding environment. Response is a necessity, the mother/child interactions being the original 'set' for this circulation. The *play cue* is the lure or invitation from the child to the surrounding environment to join in play productions of one sort or another. The playworker, when interacting with the child, albeit at later developmental stages, is required to respond to these cues in a variety of ways. Understanding this process largely informs the intervention strategies we go on later to discuss.

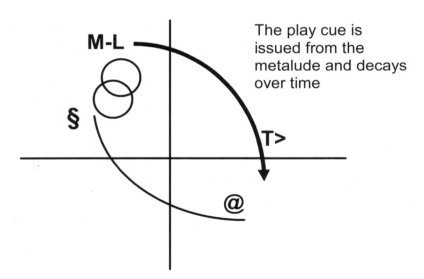

M-L

§

T>

@

The play cue is issued from the metalude and decays over time

If we conclude that play is a form of consciousness, the play cue is the signal for the world to engage with the child's developing sense of self and reality – 'things as they are'. From the responses or constructions thus generated, the child's formational life-world evolves. The notion of

---

88 Gordon Sturrock and Stephen Rennie (1997), unpublished writings

the self and world thus combining as an entity, seen as the 'integra', has some charm. This leads to our generalised proposition that the individual's sense of reality, their identity and idea of the self, the integra, are formed out of their play constructions. The play process is, accordingly, a vital part of human development. Sidoli and Davis, suggest the importance of the play constructed life-world when they say that:

> 'Playing and pretending are like a halfway house between inner and outer reality. This leads on to play and to imagine a playground in the mind and on to the adult capacity to give the inner playing and imagery an outer form in terms of enriched work and living. It could be said that the quality of life depends on how far we are able to play out and live what is within us.'[89]

As playwork has not attributed to the play process this level of potency, it is therefore vital that we reconsider the effects of intervention and involvement in the play of the child. Our very presence may have some impact throughout the cycle, but at some stages it becomes more critical than at others. In the earliest phases of the playing process, for example, after the period of decay, destruction or annihilation, the child is exposed and vulnerable while they issue play cues to enjoy the commencement of the next build up in the playing cycle. The cue may not be a positive prompt. It could be the issuance of emotion or anxiety. It may be seen as attention seeking or misbehaviour. The concerned playworker should be able to read and respond to all these cues in a manner appropriate to this interplay. Play cues are issued with the expectation of response or return and when this does not take place, frustration occurs; the play cycle can become corrupted or aberrant. It is this aberrant or hybrid cycle that is the source of *dysplay*.

The issued play cues, the driven aspect of the child's play behaviour is not simply dissipated energy. It is a form of seeking, of issue and return, it is a feedback loop. For the greater part this cycle is self-supporting and ordinated. The regulatory influence of the playworker is therefore in attendance to the wider containing enclosures of play. The containment setting is variable, it can be a narrative, a theme, or a physical area, such as a den or hidden concealed space, that may need to be preserved or re-ordered so to as to offer the necessary return. On other occasions, the thread of play may require some strengthening or involvement. This might be the physical re-ordering of a setting, a metaphor, a narrative construct, a theme developed, an adjudication and so on. For example, the child may want to play 'cops and robbers'; the worker acts out the fantasy to complete the return. The seeking nature of the play cue may last from a moment to a month. The playworker must have a repertoire of responses to the play cue if they are to work effectively in the child's playspace.

---

[89] Sidoli and Davis (1988), *Jungian Child Psychotherapy*, Karnac Books, London UK

**Play Return**

In existing playwork practice, there has been a necessary concentration on physical practicalities. This priority may need to be greatly enlarged. We contend that part of the playwork task is to evaluate the playground and all its artefacts in their potential to provide *return* for the child's play *intentions*. Are the structures, as well as offering challenge, designed and built so as to provide potential for intimacy, for concealment, can the children be 'hidden'? Is the art, the representations on the walls, surfaces, the colours, motifs, and the potential for meaning that they hold, properly considered? Are they iconic? Is there space for the child's own adaptions and contributions? Is the play fruitful and fulfilling; is the full expression of the play cycle being met? Are the meanings that the children seek capable of being held and developed by the staff? Are the workers able to amplify this meaning? Are the 'meanings' that emerge from the children's play their own and not those of the staff?

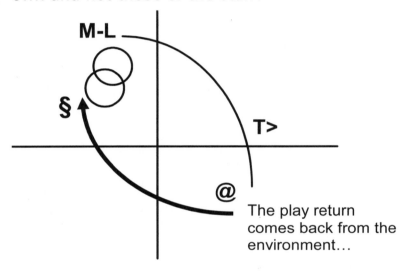

The play return comes back from the environment...

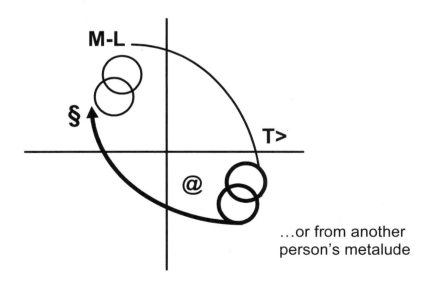

...or from another person's metalude

There can be no absolute description for effective play return. It is a condition that will always be in flux and movement. That only means that we, as part of our working practice, should develop an awareness of its continuance, being able to form, *moment to moment*, judgements about our involvement in the play cycle. All these statements are undoubtedly abstract. It can, however, be appreciated in the general ambience of the playground or play site and in the expectations of the children who elect to show up day-to-day. The final word might be left to Miles Davis as a kind of aphoristic consideration for our task. He said:

'*Don't play what's there, play what's not there.*' [90]

## Dysplay

*Example of child X:*

He always starts well, comes in good form. He gets bored, has a short attention span. He finds it difficult to wait to get involved in a game etc.

When he flips without warning

He hits other children

Uses bad language

Steals

There is one boy he gets on especially badly with. He spends a lot of time on his own. [91]

Where the cycle of play is greatly disturbed, terminated or contaminated, where the child, for whatever reason, is 'stuck' in one or other of the play loop's operative contexts, there is the possibility of dysfunctional or hybrid forms of play beginning to emerge. We term this *dysplay*. In essence, the child or the group of children are unable, for whatever reason, to play out, fully to express the meaning of their particular play. The full cycle of play is not being engaged. The play process can be used as a diagnostic tool where this dysplay can be observed. We cite one potentially controversial example of our formula being applied here.

There is a myth of the hyperactive or ADD (Attention Deficit Disorder) child being advanced. in response, we offer an assessment based on the methodologies thus far advanced.

The hyperactive child is stuck in the metaludic/annihilation (M-L. T>) phase of the ludic cycle, in what we term a 'hybrid' or 'false' cycle. They issue play cues to the containing environment as indicators of their commencing internalised gestalts. These are not picked up in the time the child allows. The return cannot be framed, and either merely

---

[90] Miles Davis (1995), as quoted in *Zen Diary*, Workman Publishing, NY, USA

[91] Bob Hughes (1996), as quoted from, *Reflective Analytic Playwork in Northern Ireland*, training notes, PlayEducation, Ely, Cambs. UK

dissipates or prematurely returns and is annihilated. The child re-issues the cues, now laden with increasing anxiety. These then repel the possibility of shared gestalt (because other children or the worker sense that something is 'wrong' and do not play), and return to annihilation (T>), before the internalised gestalt can be fully, or meaningfully explored. The complete play cycle is truncated and the whole activity becomes speeded up.

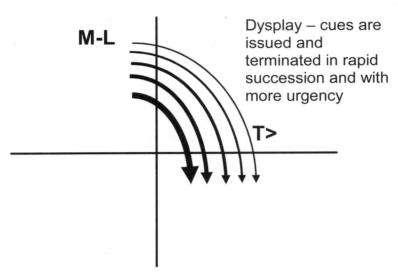

Dysplay – cues are issued and terminated in rapid succession and with more urgency

M-L

T>

Our experience shows that intervention by a sensitive playworker, where the so-called ADD child, assured that the cues were being understood and responded to, were able to frame their play and the emergent gestalts of the third phase, projective action (@), were entered into. They then enacted through the loop and flow (§), the full play cycle. As an almost immediate result, the firing off of cues, the hyperactivity, slowed down and adjusted to normal periodicity.

This application discusses only one possibility but there are any numbers of other examples that may be appropriate. Playworkers should be able to use the play cycle to underpin their understanding of the play process and accordingly make their interventions and judgements within these referential frameworks. But there remains a general point to be made about the efficacy of playwork in its encounter with unplayed out or unexpressed material that may go on, in our theoretical stance, to effect the core of neurotic formation.

In the interim we pose the following questions – given what we have said, and go on to say about the play habitat and ecology – should the issue of ADD/hyperactivity, be regarded as dysplay and as a problem of the ludic environment? Could the insights of playworkers be applied to a more widely understood neurotic dysfunction with ameliorating results?

## Adulteration

*'One does not dream with taught ideas.'* [92]

Gaston Bachelard

Due to one of the key elements of the play interchange (that is, the entry of the adult into a *gestalt mutuality*, the shared space of the narrative, theme, idea, shape, rules, games and constructs, of the child or group of children at play), the adult enjoys certain power and privilege. This is conferred by status, position, experience, authority, culture, size and society. A crucial element of the work of the playworker is the recognition of this dominion in the reflective continuum of play practice. There is a danger that the play aims and objects of the children become contaminated by, either the wishes of the adult in an urge to 'teach' or 'educate', simply to dominate, or by the worker's own unplayed out material. This latter, subtle and invidious form needs to be discussed. The attraction to many of the work may be that they have, themselves, *unworked out play material* that they feel impelled to express. This was certainly the case in our own experience. Here the frame of the child's play comes to focus on the unplayed out material of the playworker's own history and past, the children solely bit players, second bananas, on the stage of the playworker's drama or narrative.

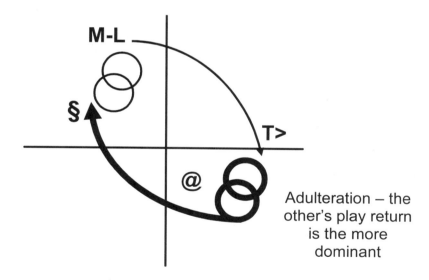

Adulteration – the other's play return is the more dominant

There is a danger of a multifold contamination in this situation. On adventure playgrounds we can see it in the grandiose structures built by some workers that become 'too good to play on,' their pristine preservation overriding the de-constructive aspects of the play cycle. Or, more abstractly, where the play themes or narratives are presented

---

[92] Gaston Bachelard (1993), as quoted in *Playing by Heart*, HCI. Publications, Deerfield Beach, Florida., USA

solely by the workers. A further adulteration is evident in the form of 'infantile toxicity'. Here the playworker becomes drawn into the child's play frame and becomes over-involved in the play. It can be seen in squabbling over 'turns', physically dominating or competing, over-complex rules, resistance to the decay of a play form and so on. Containment is neglected. The adult stands directly in the play frame. A reversal has taken place; the children now contain the play frame of adult practitioner. Where this occurs the frame of the child's play is entirely polluted by the playworker's conscious or unconscious wishes and desires.

Part of the work practice should therefore concentrate on the emotional and affective modulations that exposure to extended contact with the higher metaludic exchanges of the play process involve and the danger of potential adulteration. The playwork group as a matter of normal course should accept that they are required to use each other as a team to reflect on, analyse and evaluate, interplay exchanges in general – and in particular, where they see contamination beginning to appear. It is not bad that these phenomena can occur; it is, if we do not place them in the context of mature, corrective reflection. Containment for our practice is as important as it is for play!

## Association and Amplification

'Psychotherapy takes place in the overlap of two areas of playing, that of the patient and that of the therapist. Psychotherapy has to do with two people playing together. The corollary of this is that where playing is not possible then the work done by the therapist is directed towards bringing the patient from a state of not playing into a state of being able to play.' [93]

Should the playworker practice in what we maintain is a *reflective continuum*, then there is a need for a method that can follow the deepening of the play event into more empathic play experiences. We suggest a notion broadly borrowed from analytical psychology, namely, *association and amplification*. Samuels, *et al*, describe its Jungian use, as:

'...part of Jung's method for interpretation (particularly of dreams). By way of association *he tried to establish the personal context of the dream; by way of* amplification *he connected it with universal imagery. Amplification involves use of mythic, historical and cultural parallels in order to clarify and make ample the metaphorical content of dream symbolism... Jung speaks of this as 'the psychological tissue' in which the image is embedded.' [94] (our emphasis)

---

[93] D.W. Winnicott (1992), as cited

[94] Andrew Samuels et al (1987), *A Critical Dictionary of Jungian Analysis*, RKP, London UK

If the word 'dreams' is replaced by 'play' then the point of the quote becomes clearer. An element of the associative playwork task may be to 'make ample' the imagery, ideas and symbols of the child's enacted play. It is likely that these forms will extend well beyond the narrow cultural base upon which much present play practice is constituted. The playworker's immersion in this extended metaphoric range and the ability to enlarge it through amplification becomes a crucial component of good practice.

Most playgrounds are situated in areas where there are many cultures in place. The established idea of 'equal opportunity' in playwork has been only primitively understood and should be challenged. As an example, a playground could be seen to be meeting this need if it celebrates Diwali as a festival. Our own experience has shown that the play of children from the Indian sub-continent, Hindu and Muslim, uses images, ideas, metaphors, narratives and games that are born out of their particular culture and life-world. (The point we make here is universally applicable to children; we use these particular cultural examples solely to illustrate the point of practice.) The need for containment and return may well reside in the amplification, through the particular culture, of the material being presented. If we fail to recognise this material or to terminate or contaminate it with overlaid Eurocentric content, we rupture both the frame and return needed for effective play.

It is legitimate that we can analytically interpret a situation, where a child may be representing through symbolic form, matters, images and aspects of their emerging consciousness. An understanding of this material adds to the ability of playworkers making judgements about play intervention and the content of the child's play. This approach may also have a significant import on the organisation of the environments within which we work with the children. It may, for example, permit us to evolve a more meaningful context for descriptions of equal opportunity than the necessary but limited protocols we have up till now developed. True equality of opportunity, certainly within the play context, lies in the fullest possible exploration of the child's developing consciousness through the various symbolic and mythic forms it may give utterance to, or create. The Hindu or Muslim child may well be playing out symbolic, and other material, which has in their own cultures been met by rites and rituals. Intuitively we have known this – by recruiting workers from similar cultures, we have helped in responding to the child's needs, cultural and symbolic. By extending our own knowledge, we are able to help children from all cultures with playful expression.

## Authenticity

*'A new angelology of words is needed so that we may once again have faith in them. Without the inherence of the angel in the word – and angel means originally 'emissary,' 'message-bearer' – how can we utter anything but personal opinions, things made up in our*

*subjective minds? How can anything of worth and soul be conveyed from one psyche to another, as in a conversation, a letter, or a book, if archetypal significances are not carried in the depth of our words?'* [95]

Directly out of the idea of association and amplification comes the need for the playworker to give some thought and consideration to the responses that they issue within the play frame. Here the adult practitioner does not stand as some representative of the community or society at large. They are more vitally individuals with a responsibility to speak accurately about their feelings, ideas, affects and vulnerabilities. The playing children will come to trust the 'truth' of these responses. The repertoire of response to the child at play from the attendant adult is dependent on the faithfulness of the adult's feelings at any given time, rather than adult platitudes.

It is, for example, legitimate to express feelings of anger or dismay over an act. Both the child and the playworker can continue in the knowledge that they are not 'liked' or even 'hated' from moment to moment. Winnicott's construction of the 'good enough' mother has useful currency for play practice. He discusses the paradox of this love/hate relationship – one that should also be our own – with his usual lack of mawkishness. About mothers and children, he said:

*'Let me say quickly that I'm not talking about sentimentality. You know the kind of person who goes about saying. 'I simply adore babies.' But you wonder, do they love them? A mother's love is a pretty crude affair. There's possessiveness in it, there's appetite in it, there's a 'drat the kid' element in it, there's generosity in it, there's power in it, as well as humility. But sentimentality is outside it altogether and is repugnant to mothers.'* [96]

The corollary to this deepening of our practice, examining the affective modalities within which the work is carried out, means that we must consider the dynamics of the team operative in the play context. Playwork has up till now greatly underestimated the staff working group as the locus of psychodynamic potential. Here lies the setting for the containment of our own working practice. The group, through deliberative analysis of the children's play, and their individual and collaborative responses to it, can begin to provide the proper reflective continuum for the ongoing practice. It is out of this essential peer group interplay that the judgement and intervention considerations should be essayed. This is obviously a large point, that can only be sketched here, but we wish to highlight an aspect we hold to be crucial. There can be no immersion in the symbolic depths of play if the team are not themselves prepared, by education, training and disciplinary schooling, to enter into an exploration of their own counter-responsive attitudes and feelings about play content. The *authenticity* of the worker's

---

[95] James Hillman (1995), *Revisioning Psychology*, Perennial Library, Harper Row, New York, USA

[96] D.W. Winnicott (1993), *In Search of the Real*, Jason Aronson Inc, Northvale, NJ, USA

responses is crucial to the care-giving elements of playwork practice – it is out of these abstract and intangible contributions that trusting relationships are built. It is this compact, trust between the staff, that is a major contributory factor.

## Before and After Play

*'The main idea which I acquired …which I found extremely stimulating, was to do with the part played both in neuroses and in ordinary living by a disturbance in the capacity for reflective thought, particularly in this area of the relation between reverie and directed thinking.'* [97]

The description of play that we begin to outline in this paper is definitionally structured in a more contemplative or meditative form. This is deliberate. There is a clear need for reflective periods both preceding play work, and afterwards, where the potential for the many kinds of interference with the 'emerging programme' and the child's space to play, both physical and psychic, can be discussed and dialogued. This period of free association about the nature of the playground's children is the continuance of the reflective method.

The position of the worker in the play of the child should be out of the most careful consideration of their influence, involvement and intervention. For these reasons, we see the pre and post play session briefing and de-briefing as being a crucial element of play practice. We may need to adhere to the ancient dictum of Anacharsis when he said: 'Play that you may be serious.' [98]

It is well understood that prior to the child's arrival at the play setting or site, that there will be some preparatory work ensuring the safety and security of the space at all levels. Up to now within playwork practice this preparation has been concerned solely with the physical aspects of the site, and is already well established. We make little comment about these elements within this paper. We are more concerned with other less tangible levels and interactions.

We propose that this existing preparatory and post-session range should be extended to consider certain themes, emotional acting-out, moods, created rituals, games or other constructed play forms, both physical and imaginal, with which the children have been absorbed. This could be seen as being a kind of meditative preliminary to engagement with the playing encounter to come. These sessions should allow staff to examine the catalogue of their own particular responses to the play themes, ideas and symbolism that occur. The amplification and associative richness of the playworker's responses, the potential for return, can be greatly enhanced by use of these sessions. In addition,

---

[97] Marion Milner (1992), *The Hands of the Living God*, Virago Press, London

[98] Anacharsis, as quoted in (1994), *The Quotable Play Therapist*, Jason Aronson Inc, Northvale, NJ. USA

there exists the necessary safe space, the group's trust and confidence in each other, for the more negative implications of the work to be aired.

All this naturally applies to the kind of reflective continuum that follows the play session. Presently, afterplay is normally considered to be extra-curricular to the main playwork task. We see it vital that it is considered as a crucial element of the job and, as such it should be included as essential to the core practice. Both are as important as face-to-face work. To 'de-brief' from play with the child is a form of sanative cleansing for the playworker.

## Understanding

*'Your clear eye is the one absolutely beautiful thing*

*I want to fill it with colour and ducks*

*The zoo of the new*

*Whose names you meditate...*

*April snowdrop, Indian pipe,*

*Little.'* [99]

The various forms that we advance within this paper should not be seen as being firm protocols or procedures for involvement. We would prefer that they act simply as a framework for what is the core of our activity; namely, to understand the play of the child, through contact with that play. This necessitates an acceptance of play as multiformed and as having depth and significance. Is the sense of play that we set out not to do with the developmental complexity of identity and self and all that that entails?

Might it not be a truism that in our playwork practice we provide a framework, the necessary, reflective containment, for the child as he or she expresses their hurts and highs, their dramas and delights? Are we not acting as the mediums for this expression, bringing perhaps the unthinkable into the light for it to be safely given life and played out? This element of our practice, could have significant parallels with the description that the psychiatrist, Stanislav Grof, offers, when he says:

*'Whatever the nature and power of the technique used to activate the unconscious, the basic therapeutic strategy is the same: both the therapist and the client should trust the wisdom of the client's organism more than their own intellectual judgement. If they support the natural unfolding of the process and co-operate with it intelligently – without restrictions dictated by conventional conceptual, emotional, aesthetic, or ethical concerns – the resulting*

---

[99] Sylvia Plath (1993), 'Child' from *Poems on the Underground*, Cassell Publishers, London, UK

*experience will automatically be healing in nature.'* [100] (our emphasis)

In the above statement if 'child' and 'playworker' replace the words 'client' and 'therapist' we arrive at a meaningful description of playwork. Material emerging, as it must, out of the unconscious of the child or children at play is not unformed, non-representative imagery. It can be seen to conform to a whole range of collective, mythic material that is transpersonally – that is across cultures and races – pertinent to our human developmental processes. Ken Wilber insists: 'Development – or evolution – consists of a series of hierarchical transformations or unfoldings of the deep structures out of the ground unconscious.' [101] The playworker sits, precisely, in connective relationship with the child's *ground consciousness*.

Part of the great task facing our discipline is to arrive at the point where the adult worker can address the essential exchanges of play 'without restrictions'. A kind of attending that can only be reached by extensive reflection on our pasts, our persons and our practice, what Grof means by 'co-operate with it intelligently'. Playwork, at any level, must come to terms with this form of endeavour as fundamental to our practice. It is within a web of relationships, of the most crucial, formative kind, where the work of play begins. It is in service of these tentative and difficult interactions that the dynamic processes of the work take shape. Playgrounds, playworkers and children, all interact to create containers of meaning for the playing child, moment-to-moment, day-to-day.

## Some Operative Constructs: Methods of Involvement

*'My nature is subdued to what it works in,*
*like the dyer's hand.'* [102]

Shakespeare

We offer the following precepts as a preliminary analysis of operative involvement in the play of the child or children. In general they can apply to both individuals and groups. They do not represent a taxonomy, a classification for play; rather they are a kind of reflective prompt for what should be a more generalised and wider contemplative stance on the acts and actions of playing.

Interventions themselves can be understood in the following hierarchy:

### i) play maintenance:

> The children at play are absorbed in the acts or fantasies of play, the play is self-contained. The reading that applies will be of the traces that the children might leave, the drawings, created or used objects, toys, the resulting narratives, rules and rulings, rituals or

---

[100] Stanislav Grof (1985), as cited.

[101] Ken Wilber (1989), *The Atman Project*, Quest Books, Wheaton Ill. USA

[102] Shakespeare, as quoted in (1995), *Zen Diary*, Workman Publishing, NY, USA

rites. There is an appreciation of content but minimal contact. The playworker is mindful of the frame and the overall containment aspects of the play and ensures that the play can continue without undue interruption, but is otherwise passive. There is no overlap of involvement in the play.

### ii) simple involvement:

Following the issued play cues of the child, the adult acts as a resource for the play. This might include materials for the extension of expression, paints, clay, paper, brushes, tools, toys or some other hardware. The playworker serves solely and only in the supply elements of play. The playworker is mindful of the frame of the child's play, that is the most immediate area of their involvement, and that of their wider containment, but there is no overlap or other than a momentary involvement in the play as a material resource.

### iii) medial intervention:

Following the issued play cues of the child, the playworker becomes involved in the essential structures of the play. The immediate frame of the child's play now includes the presence/ideas/wishes/ knowledge/authority and status of a playing adult. The playworker is reading this frame, and their involvement, at the same time as being a playing participant. This role requires a kind of duality of thinking where the worker is both active in the play and 'witnessing' the various enactments of the ongoing exchanges.

The underlying play strategy is one where the structure, that is the frame of play, is partially created by the worker and the children together. Once this most intangible but necessary frame is in place – it can 'hold' the imaginal play of the children – the worker can withdraw and once more attend primarily to containment. The timing and duration of this involvement should be sensitive to the need for this arrangement to be set in place. It is therefore crucial that the worker not be bound by a crude understanding of time but by the essential needs for secure space for play framing to occur. There is a direct overlap in the play of the playworker and the child.

### iv) complex intervention:

In complex intervention, there is a direct and extended overlap between the playing child and the playworker. The forms of play, gestalts or otherwise, are shared and, though still functioning in the 'witnessing' position, the playworker is enmeshed in the interplay with the group or individual. The strategy within this form of play is the same as in medial play, but the clear judgement of the worker, in this context, is that the frame and the content of the play may involve complex material or expression and be of an extended nature. Again, the use of the term 'extended' does not refer solely to time or duration. The judgement of the worker is that the internalised, gestalted emergent forms of play merit their ongoing involvement. This 'call' is more pertinently to do with a reading of the play flow, the ludic process and the child's journey through that process, rather than termination or exit. The playworker is taking a measure of depth as much as passage.

The crucial judgement that pertains is that the playworker is there to co-operate with the symbolic and other material that the children are issuing and expressing, helping them find a frame that can effectively hold the meaning of their play, with and for them. For the main part, the children will be able to do this for themselves. On occasion, however, the self-explorative exposure of hitherto unexpressed material or content may require the playworker to help its meaning to be fully played out.

The playworker could be seen to stand as the *mid-wife* to the child's play productions. For we must bear in mind that:

*'The creation of something new is not accomplished by the intellect, but by the play-instinct acting from inner necessity. The creative mind plays with the object it loves; '...we know that every good idea and all creative work are the offspring of the imagination, and have their source in what one is pleased to call fantasy...' the dynamic principle of fantasy is play.'* [103]

### v) the integrity of intervention:

The playworker may be involved in any number of disputed or conflicting frames, narratives, themes and games, and so on. The children themselves may be at a number of stages in the process, with the frame itself being contested by differing factions. There may be calls for rulings, settlements, or re-establishment of a theme that has been eroded, changed or forgotten. The worker may be dealing with individuals and groups of children who are different levels in their discrete play frames. There will be pressure on the worker's time and involvement. The lively actions of some may be mitigated by the need for quiet rapport with others. There may be an active collusion to 'test' or distract the worker.

Throughout the maelstrom of activity and demand, the playworker is making and issuing judgements. Though this has previously been tacitly acknowledged, currently there is no method or construction around which the playworker can perfect this methodology. The danger is that these judgements and the worker's involvement can drift into personal and localised subjectivities. The various frameworks we have outlined attempt to alleviate this tendency. They offer the proposition that the playworker can be *subjective* about the playing child and *objective* about their practice. They are not protocols or procedures – rather they should be seen as guideposts for the worker's presence in the play exchange.

The various methodologies we develop in this paper are intended to maintain the integrity of playworkers in their many onerous tasks. They

---

[103] CG Jung, *Collected Works*, Vol. VI

are at work in a continuum of judgement and intervention beyond the scope of many other disciplines in terms of its potential for good or for harm. The playworker is present in the creation of the self, in work that is of the deepest psychological promise; and perhaps the soul of the child. A task we are required to re-think, just as Hillman, advises that we may be required to re-think psychological work more generally:

> 'If soul-making is not treatment, not therapy, not even a process of self-realisation but is essentially an imaginative activity of the imaginal realm as it plays through all of life everywhere and which does not need analyst or an analysis, then the professional is confronted with reflecting upon himself and his work.' [104]

## Conclusion

> 'Then out at last: the streets ring loud and gay,
> and in the big white squares the fountains play,
> and in the parks the world seems measureless,
> And to pass through it all in children's dress,
> with others, but quite otherwise than they...' [105]

Rainer Maria Rilke

In one of his sagest pronouncements, C. G. Jung, said, "the greatest sin is to be unconscious". Might we not say the same about the practice of playwork? Is there any other discipline, where vital questions about the medium within which the work is conducted, are so little asked, or so partially answered? Are we not operating without due care and attention being paid to the more hidden aspects of our task? Are playworkers actively involving themselves in the dynamic processes of the child's play without a real understanding of its inherent worth, or of the effects of their interventions? Might we not be, rather like the Idris Shah tale of the little fish who asks with some puzzlement of his mother, "What is this sea that everyone talks about?" Should playworkers now begin to reflect on the 'sea of play' in which we are all swimming?

So, we wish to suggest a puzzle, a kind of *koan* of play. (The koan is a statement from out of the traditions of Zen Buddhism that serves to distract the everyday workings of the mind, permitting new dimensions of understanding to emerge; 'what is the sound of one hand clapping', being one well known example.) Our koan seeks not to ask the question; 'what is play?' Rather we insist on a smaller more intimate question; namely, *'what is it that this play is*?' It is out of this question, gently posed of the playing child that the playwork task evolves.

Playworkers, in the play paradigm we have outlined, are required to work with myriad forms of play, from the grossest to the most subtle, with emergent, sometimes symbolic material. They work in a variety of

---

[104] James Hillman (1992) *The Myth of Analysis*, Perennial Library, Harper Row, New York, USA

[105] Rainer Marie Rilke (1996), 'Childhood', from *Rilke, Everyman's Pocket Library*, David Campbell Publishers, London, UK

interlocking frames, with an interrogative, self-questioning rigour, an extended consciousness of the ludic and the ability to respond from a wide metaphoric and narrative range. This might appear to be daunting were it not for the fact that much of this methodology exists in the 'tacit knowledge' of playwork. It is already much considered in the many extra-mural discussions that follow play sessions and is beginning to be seen in playwork discourse more generally. We have simply attempted to offer it some form and shape. Given what we perceive as being the state of play more widely, we feel it is of increasing importance that we do so.

We would argue that we need created playgrounds as the original and infinitely more rewarding natural grounds for play are being eradicated, contaminated or developed for adult purposes. The play habitat, physical and non-physical, is thoroughly adulterated. Nowadays, it must be recognised, when we provide a play environment we do so as a substitute provision. Playwork therefore functions within forms of containment that are artificial. And, if the argument is that playgrounds are unnatural (or compensatory), then it follows that we must make sure that the stuff that goes on within them, our day-to-day, adult, involvement, is as child centred and sensitised as we can manage. We need to acknowledge that we function within a *recreated* space – one that mirrors a deeper and more profound naturally occurring pastoral of the child at play in the environment.

The governance of this space, both physical and psychic, means, for the first part, that those involved in playwork must have deep insights into their own histories and habits. And, that we accept that the playground functions as a container of meaning for the playing child; meanings, which, from time to time, we may be required to interpret and decode out of these insights. We feel that the task of playwork requires us to operate in a continuum of judgement and intervention in what is a precious and internal ludic ecology; namely, that of the child at play. A methodology, or mode of practice, to which we have given too little attention, at a time when alternate designs that promote content interference in the play process, which may actually harm the child, are enjoying a certain credibility, it is appropriate to offer something other. Some of the internalised, fantasy material emerging out of a child's play may not fit into practice structured around programme, conditioning, or control, but it must be expressed!

It is perfectly acceptable to suggest that the child on the playground is an actor in an imaginal theatre of their own construction. Their passage through some of this ludic material will on occasion require a series of interventions and judgements by the playworker. If the child is in a cycle of play where the playworker sees some of the patterning we have described being enacted, where there may be the first signs of obsessive retentive play, it may be that a sympathetic ritual or rite can be enacted that will allow this passage to be safely negotiated. That this engagement can draw on a knowledge of myth, ethnography and anthropology, and some of the analytic, interpretative material, so abundantly available in the depth psychologies, seems to us to be route worth exploring. A field of knowledge with insights that could impact directly on that threshold area out of which we essay our judgement calls. Judgements, we reiterate, that playworkers are required to make in a context and continuum that is more onerous than almost any other profession. One that has a weighty contributory effect on the child's development and well-being.

The profound irony that holds might be that the play adventure is no longer simply in the physical risk but also, and perhaps more crucially, in psychic risk. We may be involved in supporting the child in undertaking arduous and difficult self-explorations or expressions with us in attendance. Ludic acts are played out in the containment of the play setting or playground where the child re-inscribes unconscious content within new individuated, ecological constellations. The 'readings' that we are obliged to make of such playful enactments can be enhanced by our understanding of those themes and symbols, common across the developmental bands, that we encounter in our growing and evolving, human consciousness. That play should have a significance for ecological well-being seems to us to be without question. Playworkers could advance a new form of therapeutic endeavour that is not enshrined in the privilege of the adult practices but abides in the play of the child. Were we to seek an explanation of this new work and its purpose, a last word from Ken Wilber, might suffice, he noted:

> 'A person's growth, from infancy to adulthood, is simply a miniature version of cosmic evolution. Or, we might say, psychological growth or development in humans is simply a microcosmic reflection of universal growth on the whole, and has the same goal: the unfolding of ever higher-order unities and integrations.' [106]

**Gordon Sturrock and Perry Else**
1998

---

[106] Ken Wilber (1989), as cited

# Practical Applications of the Psycholudic Model for Play Work

Perry Else

*'The playworker is the expert in a childhood that is perfected around the transcending of biological nature and is a co-present executor in the acquisition of cultural legacies.'* [107]

Gordon Sturrock

## Scene Setting

### Three blind children and an elephant

Imagine that three blind children are playing in a zoo and they find a friendly elephant. The first grabs the elephant's ear – "It's a bat!" she cries. The second touches the trunk; "No it's a snake!" The third child finds the elephant's tail and says, "You're both wrong, it's a donkey." Looking on the scene, we would see why they think they are right and know that they were all wrong.

I feel a similar confusion when play workers begin to debate the question of what is play. Play is a complex process; different people see different things. Some of us see different things at different times. We all tend to describe what we see from our different perspectives, using different language and different metaphors. Perhaps we are like the children in the zoo, all right but also all wrong. The approach that I describe in this paper builds on work Gordon Sturrock and I have done together,[108] and is an attempt to see all parts of the play phenomena as a coherent whole in what we describe as a psycholudic model.

## Introduction

There are many variants of the play theories described below; these descriptions are simply an example of how play is seen differently from different personal and social perspectives.[109] Each can be seen to be one aspect of this thing that is experienced as play.

---

[107] Gordon Sturrock (2002), *North of the Future – Reverie, Imagination and Fantasy as a Ludic Ecology*, Ludemos Associates, London

[108] Gordon Sturrock and Perry Else (1998), *The playground as therapeutic space: playwork as healing* (known as 'The Colorado Paper'), published in *Play in a Changing Society: Research, Design, Application*, The IPA/USA Triennial National Conference, Little Rock, USA

[109] This description is based on the integral approach as described by Ken Wilber in *The Eye of Spirit* (1997), Shambhala, Boston USA

**Play as:**

| | Personal | Impersonal |
|---|---|---|
| **Individual** | Personal expression | Behaviour |
| **Collective** | Rehearsal for adulthood | Social Control |

## Play as Personal Expression

Play as personal expression looks at play from the individual and personal perspective. This is play as affect, where the child expresses (or suppresses) their feelings to the world. It is play seen from a psychological perspective where the child creates a world of their own, or recreates it in ways that please them.

## Play as Behaviour

In contrast, play as behaviour is the impersonal individual point of view; feelings do not come into this description. This view assumes that children are individual animals needing to learn the biological skills necessary to survive in the world. Play is seen as the method for acquiring these skills.

## Play as Rehearsal for Adulthood

It is when we return to the personal but collective point of view that we see play as a rehearsal for adulthood. This view takes as its starting point that we need to get on as a group in order to survive. Play is therefore an essential way to practise our social skills and become familiar with the society in which we live. Play is seen as the way in which we as individuals internalise the external environment that is our community. The specific forms and rituals we adopt are guided by instinct but will become culturally specific.

## Play as Social Control

More recently in Western society, the impersonal collective viewpoint is becoming predominant. This is related to the 'rehearsal for adulthood' view but where that perspective allows for personal exploration, play as social control is much more concerned with 'behaviour management'. Children are needed to fulfil roles within society that are determined by their parents or other adults. Play therefore takes place in predetermined, restricted ways that guide the children's skill development in necessary ways.

[Some would argue that 'play as social control' is not play in that it is not voluntarily chosen, directed by the child with no aim or reward. However, we can recognise that this form of playcare-work has become a dominant view in the UK and has attracted considerable government support.]

## What is it that Play is?

So, what is it that play is? We can recognise some of these viewpoints in what is current in the practice of playwork and the phenomenon that is play. We can also accept that as individuals we may have argued different aspects at different times.

But how can we have such divergent but similar points of view for what is commonly described as play? Could it be that these views are parts of the whole that is play, like the layers of an onion that are related but distinct unto themselves? If so, what is it that is at the core of the onion; what is it that causes children – and us – to play?

## Overview – the Play Cycle

The full play cycle, as described by psycholudics (the study of the mind at play), is shown in the diagram below.

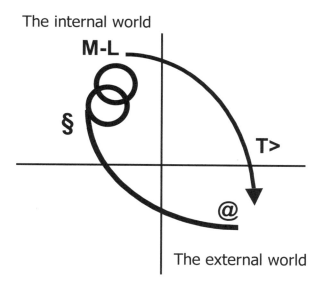

The play drive comes from the internal play source (ML) of the child, who issues play cues into the environment. Play cues will decay over time (T>) unless they interact (@) with another person or a stimulus in the environment. This play return is then processed (§) by the child, who may choose to extend the play by issuing another play cue. This is the complete play cycle. The process is described in more detail in the following sections.

## Internal Play Source

In our experience of play, we have seen children move from a game that tests their physical skill, to one that tests their friendships, to one that tests their courage, to one that tests us, the adult representative of society. And this has happened unconsciously, subconsciously and frequently in a far quicker time than it has taken to describe it – the child is playing and there are no limits!

The space where these actions come from is concerned with all aspects of the child's well being; physical, psychological, emotional and societal. This space is in constant flux between each of these states and is concerned with all and none of them, it is beyond them. We describe this place as the *metalude*. This is a technical term meaning 'changing play space' or 'play transformation space', but we feel that it is important to understand this concept to understand all that follows. Other writers have described this concept as the 'event-experience overlap', the 'imaginal zone' or, as Winnicott called it, the 'potential space'. This space would never be found in the physical brain of the child but we, as playworkers, are aware of its existence and the influence it exerts on children at play. It is the internal space where play is created and processed in the mind of the child.

Children at play are 'alive in the moment', with no concern for the past or future. Playworkers feel these moments through their experiences with children, although the external, physical evidence is slight.

The meeting between the child and the adult in any play setting involves an 'overlapping' of these moments. In some play experiences, the child's and the playworker's individuality merge to form a new, joint identity. This happens when people play together and 'get lost' in their play. Overall, this experience is a valuable and pleasant experience for all involved. However, as playworkers, we need to be aware of the potential abdication of responsibility that may happen if we become more engrossed in the play than in the work responsibility.

## Play Drive

We believe that children are *driven* to play. They will play beyond most physical and psychological boundaries – the need for food, sleep, toilet, rules, prohibitions and fears. In this sense, play challenges all the viewpoints listed above; it supports some of them but is not tied to only one of them. The play drive is the term we give to what arises in the 'internal play space' of the child. The drive is the child's urge to experience and test all that is around them. It is a necessary part of existence and the suppression of this drive causes problems for the child either immediately or later in life. Again, this has been experienced many times by playworkers in their daily role.

If the child is confident and finds someone or something stopping their play, they will usually find a way round it. This creative act may bring them into immediate conflict with an authority figure. If the child is insecure, they may blame themselves for the problem, internalise the suppression, and so stop developing an important aspect of their personality. This may not appear again for many years until the child feels confident to face the block, play through it, and consequently feel better.

## Play Ecology

The driven energy of play comes into the mind of the child before it emerges into the physical world. This play space we call the 'play ecology', the subtle play environment, a mobile, flexible space where options, ideas and themes change and adapt in contact with the surrounding and containing physical environment. It is therefore of both the internal and external worlds.

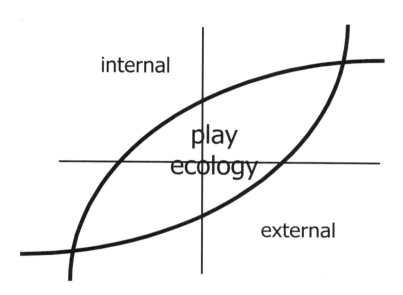

For example, play does not take place in the tools that the child uses nor in the field in which they stand. The 'game' takes place in the heads of the players; this is what we mean by the 'playful environment' (or to use our technical term, the ludic ecology). I believe it is in this space that the child measures their physical space and balances their muscles in order to move about. It is also the space where they decide on the tactics of the game, and where they will experience joy or sadness in success or loss.

## Play Frame

There are many descriptions of the importance of the physical environment for 'framing' or holding the child's play. Frequently these descriptions only look at the physical space seen by the worker. However, in any play setting there will be many play frames overlapping simultaneously and playworkers need to be sensitive to these. These frames are not just physical but involve the projected thoughts of the child at play.

In a given play setting, there will be children moving freely about the space, interacting with others, lost in their game. There will also be quiet groups of two or three individuals similarly lost in a private game or drama. There may even be a solitary individual deep in thought to him or herself. This may be the thought of joyful reflection or may be the sorrow of loss or neglect. The physical environment will be the same but the children's experiences will be different for each individual. It is this range of frames of which the worker needs to be aware; some will lead to play, others will not.

These frames can last literally seconds to many weeks. The joy (or trauma) may pass and the action will move on; or the game may be extended through many levels and depths of involvement – such as traditional den building where the play goes through scrounging, building, acting, adaptation, destruction, to name just a few of the play uses. The frame will last a long as it has relevance and meaning for the projected play form of the child.

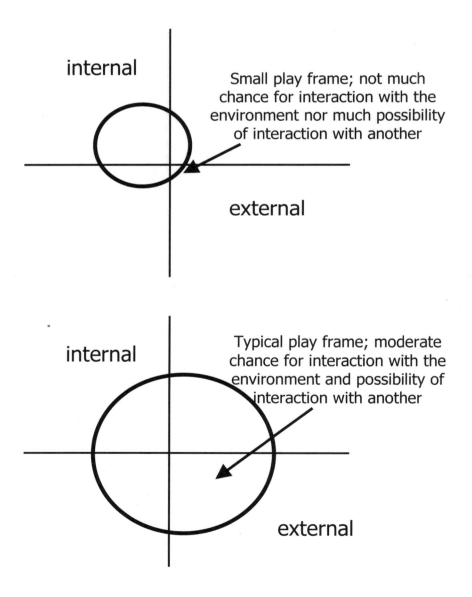

The most important function of the frame is that it provides the context or stage where the play form is made real. In healthy play, the frame is chosen and initiated by the child. It is a holder of meaning for the child and can be used as a reflector for this meaning. The play frame becomes ineffective when it can no longer provide this reflection or return. The play frame can therefore be seen as a child initiated, non-material constraint or boundary that helps define and give meaning to play content.

## Play Cues

When children are playing, they are driven to issue play cues from the play source (the metalude) and to form the play frame. The play cue is the invitation from the child to the surrounding environment to join in play of one sort or another. The play worker, in order to interact with the child, needs to respond to these cues in a variety of ways. Understanding this process largely informs how we then work with the child.

If we recognise that play is a form of consciousness, the play cue is the signal for the world to engage with the child's developing sense of self and reality – 'things as they are'. From the responses generated, the child's sense of self, their personal life-world is developed. Sidoli and Davis say this as follows; 'the quality of [our] life depends on how far we are able to play out and live what is within us'.[110] It is only by recognising this vitally important fact that we can begin to appreciate the effects of intervention and involvement in the play of the child.

The play cue may not always be a positive prompt; it could be an emotional or anxious outburst that is seen as attention seeking. The concerned playworker should be able to read and respond to all manners of cues in a way appropriate to the situation. The playworker should have a range of responses to the play cue if they are to work effectively in the child's play space (this is expanded in the next section). Play cues are issued with the expectation of response or return and when this does not take place frustration occurs; the play cycle can become corrupted. This corruption can be the source of dysfunctional play behaviours.

## Play Return

The response to the play cue is the play return. In play, the response or return may come from the environment. The child issues a playful intent that is 'reflected' by the environment, the child sees or experiences something that completes the play loop and encourages the play to continue.

---

[110] Sidoli and Davis (1988), *Jungian Child Psychotherapy*, Karnac Books, London UK

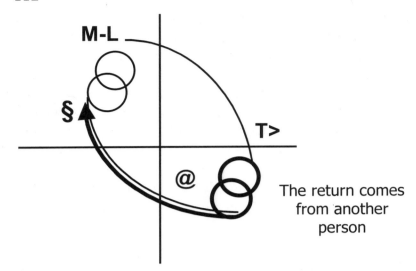

**M-L**

**§**

**T>**

**@**

The return comes
from another
person

More frequently, the return will come from another child or a playworker. The play return is the material that the playworker introduces to extend or enhance the children's play – it is the appropriate response to the various themes that the children uncover and express.

The child could be exploring its first experience of death, say after finding a dead bird under a bush. The worker can react to the child coming to share this with them in one of three basic ways. The first is to express disgust and to tell the child to 'drop that dirty thing'. The second would be to ignore the child and let them explore for themself. The third way would be to engage with the child and their curiosity and to ask and answer the 'how' and 'why' kind of questions. Only the last example will potentially extend the play; the first will stop it cold, the second adds nothing.

The challenge for us as playworkers is that we need to make these play returns 'moment to moment' as we are interacting with the children. Additionally, as has been said, there may also be several overlapping play frames in the play space and all of these will need separate and individual judgements in order to enhance the play without adulterating or inhibiting it.

### The Response – Loop and Flow

When the child gains a return from the environment, that return is 'processed' back in the internal play space, the 'play transformation space' or metalude. Again the process is far quicker than I am able to describe but goes something like this. The child responds to the cue, finds something in it of interest, decides to engage with that aspect and issues another or related play cue, which then starts the play cycle off again. The process is described as a 'loop and flow' (§) to try to capture the freedom with which the child is able to engage with any aspect of the play return. Children freely playing are capable of changing roles, rules and games within seconds.

These descriptions illustrate the complete cycle of play. Play is not just the behaviour that children exhibit when playing, nor is it solely the physical or social activities seen. Play is a much more subtle and dynamic process that requires sensitive interaction by skilled people. Many of us have known this for many years, yet our practice does not use this experience as its prime 'reason for being.' Instead, we focus on practical play skill acquisition or the safety elements of the physical environment as being more important. The psycholudic approach suggests that we need to refocus our efforts on what happens in the play cycle in order to understand its complete dynamics and the influence on developing children.

## What is not Play?

### Dysplay

The corruption of the play cycle is the source of dysfunctional play, dysplay. Dysplay can result as the breakdown of any of the three main components of the play cycle; the cue, the return and the response from the child.

In severe situations the child will simply stop playing, no cues will be issued and the child will be acting as a robot, going through the motions but without any real engagement with what is happening. Fortunately, this is rare as the child's in-built capacity to adapt and survive is one component of the drive for play.

More frequently play will cease or become corrupted when there is a poor or inadequate response from the environment or another player. This is explored in more detail below but for now the essential factor to understand is that the play cue from the child is not returned to the child. In confident, healthy children, the cue will be reissued in a slightly different way to try to engage a response. Children who may feel more insecure in the external world will tend to repeat the cue with more frequency and more alarm. These are the children who 'bother' other people, and, we believe, the children who are labelled hyperactive. These children are stuck in the play cue phase of the play cycle, repeatedly issuing cues that are not returned effectively to the child.

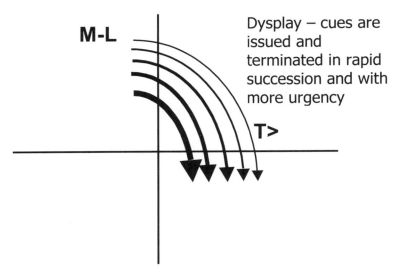

**M-L**

Dysplay – cues are issued and terminated in rapid succession and with more urgency

T>

The final stage where dysplay can occur is when the child is unable to complete the loop and flow of the play. Again, while this is usually not a problem for healthy children, some children may be so traumatised that they cannot process the response in a positive way, or they find it is safer to issue a learnt response. These children can only play one game or one role in a game. They do not have the confidence to break out of that role and in closer examination, it may be seen that they are not playing at all but are merely acting.

This is a complex process but one with which many experienced playworkers are familiar. Playworkers should be able to use the play cycle to underpin their understanding of the play process and so make their interventions and judgements within this framework.

## Adulteration

Occasionally the play framework can be misused. The playworker has power and privilege in the work environment. There is a danger that the adult contaminates the play aims and objects of the children. This can occur if the worker wants to teach or educate or, consciously or unconsciously, wishes to dominate the play. Adulteration is when the play themes are determined solely by the workers. The children are reduced to being components of the adult's play or teaching activity. It may be that the worker 'disapproves' of the child's suggested play activity and wants it to stop, or it might be that 'we are not playing that game right now; we'll do that later.' Either way the child is not being allowed to influence or contribute in a healthy way to the play process. Gordon Sturrock says this more forcefully; 'If we continue to contaminate and pollute the imagination of the child... with intrusive adult wishes, fears, aspirations and demands, we go some way to destroying the child's well being.' [111]

---

[111] Gordon Sturrock (1998), as cited above

## Controlling, Behaviour Management

It has become common to hear of playwork training methods that deal with controlling or managing children's behaviour. More recently, we also hear of homework clubs where the emphasis may be on skill acquisition at the expense of playing. In this form of adulteration, the intervention is very deliberate and is aimed at changing or modifying the children's behaviour. This is very much at odds with the commonly held understanding that play is best when it is freely chosen, spontaneous, personally directed and intrinsically motivated. An understanding of the play process shows that for the complete health of the child, play needs to be supported in a way that contributes to and enhances the play cues of the child and engages with them 'where they are.' Each child will have different needs and capacities that will need to be brought on at different rates. Not to recognise this fact is to deny the child's basic rights.

## In-authenticity

Furthermore, if the playworker is unable or unwilling to engage with the child in a clear and honest way, there is a risk of the play return being in-authentic. This may satisfy the child at first but when they realise, as they quickly will, that the response is a fake, they will rebel or learn to disrespect the worker, just as they themselves have been disrespected. More importantly, if the worker always offers a fixed response to a play cue, the children will not learn or develop.

If the worker has not worked through their own responses to situations, they will have a limited range of options with which to help the child. While not a major fault of itself, if the worker is too embarrassed to admit to this, the child may be offered an improper response; such as to drop a dead bird because it is dirty. There may be a strong, joint lesson if the worker were confident enough to say to the child, 'I don't know, let's find out'.

## Practice Applications

### Authenticity

Being honest and open with children is one of the most important things we can do with them. Part of growing up is learning to understand the difference between fantasy and reality. Keeping children cocooned in an unreal world where nothing bad ever happens will disadvantage them as they grow older. This is not a request that all children be introduced to the horrors of the world at the age of three, but it is to ask that when they show they are ready to enquire about such things that we give a mature response. It is when we corrupt their thinking by offering our own prejudices as the 'truth' of a situation that we do the greatest harm. Children need to be offered breadth and depth in the responses from the adults around them if they are to be best able to make sense of their world. It is in this way that we are best able to help children 'transcend their biological nature' and acquire their cultural legacies.

At times this may involve letting them know how upset or angry we are about what they have done; they need to see that we are human too. The child will understand far more if reprimands can be couched in terms of the problem, what was wrong, rather than a lazy, emotional outburst attacking the child as a person – 'Oh Susan, <u>you</u> always get things wrong.' Being able to be honest with ourselves is necessarily part of the need to be honest and authentic with children. This is a difficult task as it will involve us facing and challenging our own blocks, understanding those – and accordingly ourselves – could be a painful process. This is where the support of an effective play team becomes essential to the play work process.

## Reflection – Before and After Play

For several years, the playwork profession has spoken of the reflective approach to playwork. At its simplest this approach requires a regular review of the work practice to make sure that the planned programme achieved its outputs; in enlightened playworkers this reflection also includes their own behaviours and attitudes. It has become common with the introduction of the National Vocational Qualification to hear of workers reflecting in a systematic way in order to collect evidence towards their portfolio. We are suggesting a much more dynamic and integrated approach. Reflection is essential to understanding why we react to situations in certain ways. This approach recognises that the choices we make are influenced by the beliefs and attitudes we hold as well as our own emotional security (or lack of it).

The playwork team has a responsibility to help each other in this reflective task both before and after the playwork session. Again, this is something that playworkers have always done intuitively; but we are talking here about more than the pre-work coffee or post-work drink. Before work, the job is to help each other prepare for the work to come by considering what may arise in the coming session or programme. By examining how we will react to certain themes or material, we are better prepared to be a resource to the children. This preparation may include for example, consideration of the ecological impact of the activity, or how certain roles in a game carry positive or negative values. How would we help the children understand these issues; would we lecture, discuss or let the child find out for themselves? A little forethought would help supply the answers to these questions.

It may also arise that the session will produce themes and material that could not be predicted. Playworkers will then need to form quick judgements about what to do. The post-session, team reflection will help with understanding how the worker's judgement or intervention was useful. This reflection should allow staff to examine their own particular responses to the play themes, ideas and symbolism that developed in the play work session, and is particularly necessary to help with the 'acquisition of cultural legacies'. Our own perceptions will be filtered through our own particular heritage or the knowledge and events we have experienced to date. Playwork, in 1999, necessarily involves children from a wide variety of cultures and backgrounds, who may have different cultural legacies to our own. While we have now legislated for workers to accept and work with these differences, our work can be so much more than just recognition of difference. Children need workers who are culturally competent themselves, workers able to recognise the elements of a strong culture in order to support it or debate with it.

## Containment

The support that workers can give to children in play should include the ability to hold or 'contain' the play. Containment is not intended in a pejorative sense here; it is about supporting a child through their initial tentative play cues, giving back a return to help the play on its way, being 'co-present' as the child extends their boundaries. We need to remember that very little of the developed environment is 'virgin territory' for children. There is not much left that has not been 'concretised', controlled, adapted or 'made safe'. Some children need to learn how to learn skills in what is generally a hostile environment for them. The playworker gives a gentle help to the child at a critical stage, encouraging them to develop a wider play frame, one that includes as many cultural possibilities as it will hold.

Containment should also be about helping children who may be at risk of harming themselves or others. Enthusiastic children can easily extend their frame to include the whole of the environment around them; this may bring them into conflict with other users of that environment. Playworkers will need to bring the play back to a safe or tolerable level. This will necessarily involve some diminution of the play, but a sensitive playworker will be attuned to this. They will be aware of the potential for pollution or adulteration of the play cycle and will strive to satisfy the child's play drive in a culturally appropriate way. The use of rituals and rites is a valuable aid in containing play in a healthy way for children.

## Rites and Rituals

Playwork already has many rituals that we celebrate thought the day, the week and the year. The annual rituals are easy to spot, and we may be aware of the daily and weekly rituals, which will be different on each play site. Some rituals will be set by the workers, some by the children. Workers' rituals usually include a winding down activity in the last half-hour of the playwork session, or a fire or den building session at the weekend. Children will have their own initiations into various games, ways of choosing team players or challenges to prove the maturity of individuals.

Workers can extend these rituals to include positive ways of bringing games to a close, or to provide a containing context for the play until the child or children are next on the site; they provide a finalisation or completion to the play that will help the child leave the game and their role in a healthy way. Examples of this would be say putting a 'chapter ending' into a story, or agreeing that the next complete stage of the game will end it for today ('first one to score a goal').

More valuable still would be when workers help with the realisation or transcendent aspects of play and life. Workers can show children that they have 'moved on' by the use of rituals. We can help children gain in confidence when they carry out exceptional acts. For some children it may be their first appearance on stage, for others their first camp away from home, or simply the first time they were able to use a piece of equipment unaided. Recognising these acts in a formal way, rather than simply with a pat on the back, will help the child see the significance of the act and learn more from it.

I have also known some playgrounds hold a 'leaving ceremony' for young people who have outgrown the use of the playground but have not yet detached emotionally from it. The ceremony helps them make the change in a positive way, rather than feel they have been pushed out. If the ceremony is planned with the young people, they will get used to the idea of separation and be more ready for it when it happens.

## Dealing with Adulteration

It may be that a worker tries to push a child out of the play site because in their opinion the child 'does not fit'. This would be adulteration and must be challenged by other workers. The best way to deal with this would be through the reflective session before or after the play session. We need to recognise that the worker may be playing out a personal fantasy and will need release from that fantasy if they are to move on themselves.

Often simply recognising the behaviour may be enough to help them make the change, though we should be aware that at times more focused counselling might be appropriate. I am not advocating that playworkers take on this role, but being attuned to it, they can help colleagues seek out such help. Additionally, formal appraisal sessions instigated by the management team will help with the exposure or realisation of such needs. Moreover, blunt though it sounds, workers unable to change should be removed from the environment – though this is often difficult to achieve in practice.

## Environmental Implications

### Factors of a Play Enabling Environment

So far, I have focused on the efforts of the play team, but just as valuable, perhaps even more valuable, is the quality of the environment for play. As is now widely recognised, the modern environment is not play friendly. If we accept that the child can gain a play return from a play enabling environment, we are depriving them of their right to play in much of the modern environment. More frightening still, is that in the main, the defined playgrounds for children are now so designed that any sense of playfulness is completely absent – 'we are seeing the gradual diminishing of the child's right to reverie, imagination and fantasy.' [112] As a society, we tend to be obsessed with the safety of play equipment, the number of swings, their seat design and their colour. We should instead be concentrating on the quality of the environment so that it provides stimulus, fun, release, and life enhancing and therapeutic aspects.

Such an environment has been frequently described by Bob Hughes and others but to repeat it would include: the natural elements, fabricated and natural materials, challenge, movement; stimulus for the senses, opportunities for playing with identity, for social interactions, change, and overall be an interesting and varied physical environment.

## Training Implications

We have also been saying for many years that provision should also be child directed, child influenced, free to come and go, supported by sensitive adults. If this long cherished statement about play is not to be lost in the rush to turn us all into care workers or education workers, we need to say very clearly that growth, learning and ultimately, self healing, does not come through being 'force-fed' the message. I know I'm repeating what will be obvious to most playworkers but this message needs saying loud and long; education is not the way to create healthy, balanced individuals; to mis-quote the old saw, 'You can take a child to school, but you cannot make them think'.

## Natural Playworkers and Others

The person whom I call the 'natural playworker' has always understood this. The natural playworker is the balanced individual who knows how and when to intervene in the play of the child and when to leave well alone. They will have a repertoire of responses to the child when necessary that will include the ability to be controlling without being aggressive, and encourage free play without being weak or passive. To offer a quality play provision, we need to be sure that all workers have these skills.

What concerns me about the majority of our current play training is that it does not cover all the aspects of play; it does not 'see the whole of the elephant'. To extend the metaphor:

- we know how the trunk should move and think we know its capabilities (behavioural characteristics)

- we can describe the size of the ears, state their colour and texture (environmental criteria)

---

[112] Gordon Sturrock (1998), as cited above

- we have lists of appropriate tails, and lessons in how to apply them (suitable equipment)
    - but would we recognise 'the elephant' from the sum of these parts?

To come back to the point, does play training help us to know what it is that play is? Learning all the games in the world will not facilitate play if the worker leading those games is not in tune with the play cues that the children will be issuing. They will not be aiding play if they have a limited range of responses to children that offers no growth or stimulus to the cue of the child. Training offers tools that workers can use, but frequently it is up to the worker to interpret when the tool is appropriate. We support this interpretation by offering experiential learning, but again the logic is that understanding what play is, is learned by osmosis, from other, successful playworkers.

The psycholudic model is intended to be a way of making the structures of play more explicit and therefore more easily understood. Overall, we are aiming to create workers who are balanced and healthy individuals, able to make sound, culturally aware decisions.

## National Vocational Qualification Developments

We are not intending to produce workers who are merely mechanistic, who are able to show their competence across a range of quantifiable but developmentally dry topics. While the development of the NVQs have helped many individuals who are working in play gain some recognition and confidence from their long held experiences, like some training, they have not helped in the validation and description of what it is that play is. To return again to my opening story about the elephant, play is not just about, say, behavioural development. True play is also about personal expression, skill rehearsal and cultural understanding. True play work should encompass all these aspects and should encourage operation across many developmental levels. The currently available NVQs need extending to recognise these points.

## Summary

A lot of good work has been done in recent years to raise the status of play and play work. We now need to step up the pace and not be afraid to state in forceful terms what many of us have felt for years, that play is fundamental to the development of children. Play is more than a rehearsal for adulthood, more than behavioural development, more than personal expression. It is a whole that is more than the sum of its parts, and – fundamentally – it is to do with the child's developmental well-being in the widest possible sense.

There are many compelling reasons why now is the time for playworkers to assert their claim to be experts in a child's development through play. But chief amongst these is the need to understand and guard the play space, both physical and intangible, that is critical for children's self development.

Psycholudics, the study of the mind at play, is an attempt to describe the process of play so that it can be more easily understood for training and research purposes. It aims to give clear definitions of the parts of the play process so that these can be explored and debated by the playwork profession. It aims to help us see the whole picture.

**Perry Else**
January 1999

# The Impossible Science of the Unique Being [113]

Gordon Sturrock

'*Nihil est in intellectu quod non anteafeurit in sensu.*'

There is nothing in the intellect that had not first been processed through the senses.

John Locke

## Preamble

I am taking advantage of two factors in the presentation of this paper. The first, is that I have the comfort of colleagues in the symposium who will be examining and earthing much of what has passed between us all in a most interesting discourse over recent years. They allow me to venture excessive speculation. The second, is that at the last meeting of us as players prior to the end of two of numbers of millennia, I feel no need to be constrained by grounding.

Einstein it was who said that 'all science begins in myth'. What follows therefore, is a myth, one of 'those things that never happened but are forever.' I choose myth because when confronted with play and its wonder, we adults fall into a kind of monadic trance. One that spells the end of logic and an entire canon of Newtonian-Cartesian thinking. When Grof says: There is little doubt in my mind that our current understanding of the universe, of the nature of reality, and particularly of human beings, is superficial, incoherent and incomplete.' [114] I tend to agree. I ask you therefore to join with me in an exploration taking place in an 'as-if domain. What follows is not fact and, if it is fiction, I hope it is a 'healing fiction'. It is a kind of dream of play, a reverie.

'*Dreaming of childhood, we go back to the den of reveries, to the reveries, which opened up the world for us. It is reverie, which makes us the first inhabitants of the world of solitude. And we live all the better in the world, living as the solitary child lives in images. In the child's reverie, the image comes first. Experiences only come afterwards; they go against the current of all reveries of flight. The child's vision is grand and beautiful. Reverie oriented toward childhood takes us back to the beauty of first images.*' [115]

'Back to the den of reverie'. The player faces this task each day obliged to be, in the words of Rilke, 'always a beginner', engaging in the 'isness'- Eichrat's *istigkeit* captures the idea well – of the ludic's existential dimension. It is this dimension that I wish to discuss.

---

[113] From Roland Barthes, *Camera Lucida*

[114] Stanislav Grof, 1985, *Beyond the Brain*, Suny Press New York, USA

[115] Gaston Bachelard, *Reverie and Imagination*, source unknown

## Introduction

*'There was never any more inception than there is now, Nor any more youth or age than there is now And will never be any more perfection than there is now, Nor any more heaven or hell than there is now.'* [116]

In any meaningful investigation of childhood, play should form the most salient aspect of enquiry. That it does not, that our understanding of play and our adult colonisation of play goes unheeded, is a matter of some environmental consequence. It is the concept of an imaginal, ludic domain that forms the key idea of this paper. The theme is of a developmental process that we have, out of a kind of profane idea of adulthood, ignored at a certain cost. That cost can be measured in the loss of a level of civilising humanity. Recall Huizinga:

*'The view we take in the following pages is that culture arises in the form of play, that it is played from the very beginning.'* [117]

This paper is not about definitions of play. Rather it examines a locus, a perspective, an 'inscape'. The quote that precedes this paragraph is from a poem by Walt Whitman, 'Song of Myself'. So, the first part of the journey is not into a sweeping *terra incognita,* an unknown land, but into a microcosm, the microcosm of the play exchange. The interplay, between the playing child and the playing adult is where I will make my excursion and my essential confabulation.

## Games of Knowledge

There is a thrust In the UK towards increasing provision for children in settings redolent of control issues in early development. Were we to regard it as a space, rather than as a regime or operational credo, we might have a better perspective on this colonisation. For adult convenience children are being inducted into institutionalised playcare programmes. The rationale for this movement is essentially political. As centres – 20,000 over the next few years – come on stream the ethos and philosophical grounding will follow flaggingly behind. Tellingly among the first slogans for this new social engineering dynamic is the 'good enough' playworker.

Within this fairly innocuous soundbite lies a major clue as to the likely providence of a future playcare and, perhaps playwork, dialectic. As has happened in the past, we will see the bending and misapplication of theory to justify practice wedded to established paradigms in what Kuhn describes as the 'period of normal science'. In this form research will take the shape of 'strenuous and devoted effort to force nature into the conceptual boxes supplied by professional education': Kuhn again.

The one thing we may be assured of is that those who seek to underpin political dominion over hitherto free open access will always do so by

---

[116] Walt Whitman, *Song of Myself*

[117] Huizinga, *Homo Ludens*

the imposition of 'old science'. We will be forced into acceptable old paradigms of thinking. Thinking becomes a form of policing to maintain and reinforce normative aims. Grof sets out the stall:

> 'When a paradigm is accepted by the majority of the scientific community, it becomes a mandatory way of approaching problems. At this point, it also tends to be mistaken for an accurate description of reality instead of being seen as a useful map, a convenient approximation, and a model for organizing currently available data.' [118]

## The Old Rule

In the UK, there is an idea of an organising model for playwork presently being energetically pursued as just such an 'accurate description of reality'. In a recent draft document issued through the new playwork lead body, SPRITO, 'Towards a Training and Qualification Framework', the 'values of playwork' are studiously laid out. They include: empowerment, equal opportunities, extending the child's world and the play environment. These terms are not carefully defined; they are not based on meaningful research; they have no powerful underlying thesis. They are little more than a leftover language of a political agitprop platform serving the creation of a new breed of playwork apparatchik.

This 'old rule' sees the structural growth of strenuous supervision, regional councils, the establishment of Vigilance' as being the buzzwords in a new renaissance of playwork. The accompanying letter with this draft sets out the stall: 'Playwork is making history' screams the headline. It goes on to explain:

> 'Once again playworkers are at the forefront of developments that will shape the future of children's lives. As you know the government's National Childcare Strategy is making provision for a huge expansion of opportunities for children's play care and education. Up to one million new childcare places, 20,000 new out of school projects, 60,000 new playwork and childcare jobs are just some of the figures mentioned.' [119]

The agenda is clear. The issue of play and of playwork as open access provision with children making the choices about when and where they play is now consigned to the dustbin. Playwork now means the reverse, the job is now partly custodial, centred on care and principally concerned with programmes of social and other types of early education, with play as an added cosmetic spin.

This view of playing, now predominantly focussed on playcare-based playwork, sees the interactions between the adult player and the child as being the interplay of a subject – the child and an object – the adult.

---

[118] Stanislav Grof (1985), as cited

[119] *Towards a Training and Qualification Framework*, SPRITO draft document (April 1999)

In this formation, the role of the adult is as some mediator, of mores, of rules, of demeanour, of behaviour, of social codes and of learning. The playspace of the child is subjected to a kind of adult-ordinated governance. Our training, much of it to be developed through the means of vocational qualification, offers that we can have an 'objective' relationship with the child and are essentially manipulative of play. Play is seen as a medium of control ensuring the child conforms to the agendas that we create. When they do not we see the kind of sanctions operating that are redolent of exclusion and expulsion. The flunking of kindergarten is now a possibility.

Agendas of conformity are now steadily extending and we find ourselves in the situation where, unsatisfied with a hegemony over what might be termed 'education' we begin the process of 'early education', social education and a new vocabulary of terms that accrete to playcare generally. These are little more than the slogans of an ill-concealed rationale for take-over of free play and all that this meant to the child. By dint of adult convenience, particularly in the political fix of returning mothers and welfare to work measures that the UK Government insists on enacting, we can perceive the demise of a free play philosophy. That this strategy has been so wholeheartedly taken up by some of those involved in the field is a matter that requires serious debate.

Is there not a better way forward? Can we not provide alternative understandings that prompt some deeper considerations when we ponder on what we are doing to the child's playspace?

## The New Rule

Here's the new rule.

   *'Break the wineglass and move closer to the glassblower's breath.'* [120]

The mathematician Ben Goertzal discussed in a paper recently the notion that new movements commence from what he described as 'magician systems'. He went on to say that they then become surrounded by 'anti- magician systems'. The perceptions that follow are speculations on the existence of a core 'magician system' in playwork.

There is a new and, to my view, exciting area of investigation in psychodynamic therapy emerging: namely, transpersonal psychology. It is to this field that I now turn. In particular I will be examining the new fields of research into meditation and mindfulness. But, as a preliminary, I wish to discuss the idea of a zone prior to actions in play. This zone a number of colleagues and myself described as the metalude. It is in linking the idea of the metalude with nascent understandings of awareness, consciousness and meditation that I see the beginnings of a new and powerful ecological application of playwork.

---

[120] Rumi, from *A Zen Diary* (1998), Workman Press, USA

## The Metalude

> *'The basic assumption of the German gestalt school is that human beings do not perceive things as unrelated and isolated, but organise them during the perceptual process into meaningful wholes.'* [121]

I intend briefly, to explore the idea of a 'dimension' in play that is a prefiguring but always present function of the ludic process. (For a fuller but not complete description see The Playground as Therapeutic Space, Playwork as Healing, Sturrock and Else, 1998 [122])

I will deal with this without any particular allegiance to disciplines or philosophical frameworks. Deleuze and Guattari provide the rationale:

> *'The reader is invited to dynamism out (of the book) entirely, and incarnate it in a foreign medium, whether it be painting or politics. The authors steal from other disciplines with glee, but they are more than happy to return the favour. Deleuze's own image for a concept is not a brick, but a 'tool box'.* [123]

I earnestly urge readers to do the same with the conceptual tool box I offer. The discussion that follows is an outline of a reality, or perhaps more accurately a real virtuality, somewhat akin to Jung's idea of 'inner psychic reality' but linked more closely to the Tantric notions of 'maya'. In essence, I argue that prior to each and every act of playing – and of creativity more generally – lies a zone of instigation of intentionality and ideas. This is the source point of all the gestalt material that goes to constitute world-making as Lowenfeldt understands it. Cobb cites Erikson to give the idea some context:

> *'The child's world making in play is a learning process, a structuring of increasingly complex gestalten, both perceptual and linguistic, in a cultural transcendence of biological levels. This process begins with the child's very earliest experimental play with this own body, which Erikson has described, poetically and yet scientifically, as 'autocosmic play'.* [124]

Elsewhere Cobb describes this process as being 'close to the biology of thought' itself. For our play purposes we might see this locus as the generation point of those play impulses – the emerging intentionality – with which we should be preoccupied in the play process. The purpose may well be linked to evolution. Cobb again:

---

[121] Stanislav Grof (1985), as cited

[122] Gordon Sturrock and Perry Else (1998), *The playground as therapeutic space: playwork as healing* (known as "The Colorado Paper), published in *Play in a Changing Society: Research, Design, Application*, IPA/USA, Little Rock, USA

[123] Brian Massimo in Giles Deleuze and Felix Guattari (1992), *Thousand Plateaux*, Athlone Press, London

[124] Edith Cobb (1993), *The Ecology of Imagination in Childhood*, Spring Publications. Dallas. TX. USA

*'The child's urge to 'body forth the forms of things unknown' in the microcosm of child art and play bears a distinct resemblance to the morphogenesis characteristic of nature's long term history, namely, evolution.'* [125]

But, it may be more than simply evolution, we may be that we are required to consider, to give thought to the process of evolution and what I will argue is the direct link into mature and adult ludic development, namely meditation and 'mindfulness'. Consequently I would like to examine the ideas that I see as being a form of ludic consciousness.

## 'Mindfulness', 'Bare Attention' and the 'Watcher Self'

*'This seemingly impossible task is achieved through what Thera calls 'bare attention' (1972): the accurate, continuous registering at the conscious level of all events occurring in the six sensory modes – seeing, hearing, touching, tasting, smelling and thinking – without qualitative judgements, evaluation, mental comment, or behavioural act.'* [126]

My essential argument is that play, the ludic process, is the start point, the developmental heart of mindfulness. The propositions of 'bare attention' and the 'watcher self seem to me to be mightily close to the core reflective tasks of the playworker. If I might first explain the basis of mindfulness, in particular, the idea of *bare* attention', which requires some explication before returning to the task of the worker active in this delicate interaction. In the course of our everyday playwork we have become used to the idea of the child lost in some daydream or fantasy. Indeed, playwork has innate respect for this locus and the daydreaming child is allowed and encouraged fully to explore this internal imaginal activity. But, while respecting this operational reverie, we have ventured no thought as to what it might be; we have never attempted to map this territory. The supposition that it is 'merely' fantasy is overly dismissive. I believe we are required to speculate what the purpose of this introspection might be. The clue I am convinced rests in the radical new perspectives on contemplation and meditation that have emerged over recent years. As a preliminary if I might first attempt to outline the concept of 'bare attention'.

Considering mediation has existed for millennia it is a little surprising that serious investigation has only recently begun. Foremost in this field have been those concerned with what is described as transpersonal psychology. The names that most readily spring to mind are Ken Wilber, Stanislav Grof and Charles Tart. They have been responsible, along with others for opening up this entire area of endeavour. As a result there are the beginnings of profound understandings of the role and function

---

[125] Edith Cobb (1993), as cited

[126] Seymour Boorstein (ed) (1996),*Transpersonal Psychology*, Suny Press, New York, USA

of meditation and mindfulness. (For the purposes of this paper I will refer to meditation and mindfulness as being the same thing.)

Bare attention stems from the meditative practice of quietly sitting in a relaxed and comfortable posture and examining one's breathing process as we respire, in and out. Such attention appears to produce interesting results. The attention closely given to an otherwise totally unregistered activity, namely the physical action of breathing makes us:

> 'Then... create a space between life's events and the ego's reaction to events. The ego itself begins to be seen and known. Mental processes basic to the ego are sometimes seen in operation. Slowly, one becomes capable of dealing more effectively and intelligently with each life event as it occurs.' [127]

This slow concentration moves the centre of being from uncontrolled mental processes. Matters which had previously impinged on consciousness recede as another awareness comes into play. This otherness, Olaf Deatherage, from whom I draw much of this understanding, speaks of as the 'catcher self'. Deatherage describes this as the 'aspect of one's mental self which is discovered through and carries out the task of mindfulness'. [128]

Now the speculative crux of this paper. Is the child lost in imaginal play entering into a developing awareness of the kind that Deatherage and many others are talking about? It is a commonplace to hear that the child through play is establishing identity and their idea of 'self'. But, is there, prior to the projection of self and identity intentionality, a 'mental self' of the kind that is seen in the work of transpersonal psychology and, much more widely in the wisdom traditions of the East? If there were, it would obviously be of ecological import. What evidence that might describe just such an active purpose?

There is strong evidence emerging of a major ecological catastrophe in children. I speak of Attention Deficit Hyperactivity Disorder – ADHD. The disorder appears to be spreading at a rate that, were it an infectious disease, would be arousing epidemiological interest. There are at present (c.2000), 3 million children in the US so diagnosed and on the drug Ritalin™, a cocaine derivative.[129] The figure for the UK, as ever slower to respond to medical imperatives, is 110,000.[130] ADHD is a lifelong problem and has associated debilitating co-morbidities. At the moment the message from the medical profession is that there is no

---

[127] Olaf Deatherage (1996), from Boorstein (ed) *Transpersonal Psychology*, Suny Press, New York, USA

[128] Olaf Deatherage (1996), as cited

[129] Ritalin is prescribed to children with Attention Deficit Hyperactivity Disorder (ADHD), 'hyperactive children'. It slows down their responses to make them more 'manageable' for parents and teachers.

[130] According to the UK Department of Health, the number of prescriptions for the drug increased by 22% in 2002. A total of 254,000 doses were prescribed that year, twice the amount given out in 1997. (BBCi, posted 17 September 2003)

psychosocial response that can ameliorate the symptoms, hence the drug regimes I talk about.

There is some research showing that, deprived of play, rats show signs of symptoms similar to those of children with ADHD. The play drive, it would appear, when not permitted fully to explore, when suppressed by external cessation, will show signs of dysplay. The typical hyperactive, inattentive restless searching of the so-afflicted child. A fitting description of such behaviour might be; mental events jump from one event to the next with a staccato rapidity that is seemingly random and chaotic, even frightening. This is Deatherage's description of the view of the mind's processes viewed from the position of the 'watcher self'.

This leads to the key set of questions. Are we seeing the breakdown of the development of bare attention and the watcher self in children? Is the increasing contamination of the child's playspace and the loss of this element of imaginal introspection leading directly to the chaotic symptomology of the ADHD child? If this is the case what might be an ameliorating response?

Is it any longer possible to construct a playwork sensibility that avoids some of the material I speak about in this paper? Can we not create a playwork methodology that offers, as psychoanalysis has done, that the key interaction in out task happens at an interpsychic level.

Deatherage gives an answer outlining what may be a suitable therapeutic job description for the playworker: 'becoming aware of one's primary interrupting factors can be diagnostically and therapeutically significant because one can see unhealthy, habitual mental processes' [131]. The interrupting stream of everyday consciousness is a matter that we may as adults choose to deal with at our own volition. Indeed many are turning to just this type of activity. But are we simply rediscovering something that we have lost? It would be a delicious irony if we were to re-acquaint ourselves with the ludic functionality of the meditative process through interplay with the child!

## To Conclude

*'Perhaps the time is now ripe when the mystic can break the glass through which he sees all things darkly, and the rationalist can break the glass through which he sees all things clearly, and both together can enter the kingdom of psychological reality.'* [132]

If, as adults, we gaze unflinchingly at the child at play, the central motif of the ludic function, we are bound to recognise that we stand apart from its mystery. We are really, as Barthes suggests, entering into the 'impossible science of the unique being.' The mere fact of maturation has moved us away from the essence of the play function. When we enter the playful exchange, particularly as playworkers, we do so in acts

---

[131] Olaf Deatherage, 1996 as cited

[132] Olaf Deatherage (1996), as cited

of remembrance. The enigma of the encounter evolves around an engagement with the child in their 'condition of freedom'. One that as societies we appear to feel compelled to constrain with certain contaminating results.

The myth outlined in this paper could be described as being to do with the ecology of thought. In its natural and purest state we may well encounter it in the playing child. Thomas Mann's idea of 'civilised magic' has some poetic resonance. It is no accident that the playful absurdities of Zen figure around a child-like contact with the universe in a kind of ludic delirium. The fable suggests this: all contemplative acts stem from a ludic dimension to pollute this in any way leads to breakdown and dis-ease. That we are now seeing this in our children may be an inevitable conclusion. That it is part of more ruthless planetary adulteration only makes it more painful. Edward O Wilson says:

> 'I believe that in the process of locating new avenues of creative thought, we will also arrive at an existential conservatism. It is worth asking repeatedly: Where are our deepest roots?
>
> We are, it seems, Old World catarrhine primates, brilliant emergent animals, defined genetically by our unique origins, blessed by our newfound biological genius, and secure in our homeland if we wish to make it so. What does it all mean? This is what it all means.
>
> To the extent that we depend on prosthetic devices to keep ourselves and the biosphere alive, we will render everything fragile. To the extent that we banish the rest of life, we will impoverish our own species for the rest of time. And if we should surrender our genetic nature to machine-aided ratiocination, and our ethics and art and our very meaning to a habit of careless discursion in the name of progress, imagining ourselves god-like and absolved from our ancient heritage, we will become nothing.' [133]

**Gordon Sturrock**
June 1999

---

[133] Edward O Wilson (1998), *Consilience*, Little and Brown, London

# Seeing the Whole Picture
# – Playwork Content in the Playwork Curriculum

Perry Else

## Welcome

There was a Guardian newspaper advert on TV a few years ago that some of you may be familiar with. It started with a close-up picture of a male 'skin-head' pulling a face and 'getting ready for action.' Your first reaction was intended I guess to feel apprehension. The second image showed a cleanly dressed businessman clutching his briefcase. The third image was of the 'skin-head' grabbing at the man, the advert was shot to suggest a mugging. The final shot was from a distance and it showed a pile of bricks falling off a scaffold; if the skinhead had not grabbed at the man he would have been killed. The punch-line was that it was only when you saw the whole picture that you got the full story. A great way to sell papers but also a useful metaphor for what I see happening in play; we all see separate parts of the whole that is play.

Reviewing some of the commonly accepted theories of play I came across the following main categories:

- The physiological and biological approaches – children play to develop their bodies and physical skills

- The psychological approach – play is a way of dealing with trauma, play as emotion

- The cognitive/developmental approach – play as intellectual development

- The socio-cultural approach – skills and role practise for later life.

All of these theories can find evidence to prove their validity; all of them are true from a given point of view. But how can all of these theories claim be representative of the phenomenon that is play? Which one was the true theory?

In this presentation I shall introduce you to a model that gives an integrated view of personal development, I shall describe the characteristics of that model and how I feel they fit within a playwork context. Then I shall briefly explain a way of understanding play that can maximise on this approach, commenting on the implications for training and playwork as I do. I hope to leave some time for questions or clarification at the end.

## Seeing the Whole Picture – The Wilber 'All quadrant' Model

This model first proposed by Ken Wilber[134] shows how development occurs in four key quadrants that represent the interior and exterior

---

[134] Ken Wilber (1998), *The Marriage of Sense and Soul*, Random House, New York USA

worlds and the individual and collective perspectives. Healthy development occurs when growth or development occurs or is encouraged in all four quadrants.

| ARTS<br>Interior individual | SCIENCES<br>Exterior individual |
|---|---|
| Concepts | Complex brain |
| Symbols | Reptilian brain system |
| Emotion | Neural cord |
| Impulse | Neuronal organisms |
| Perception | Single celled animals |
| Sensation | Molecules |
| Irritability | Atoms |
| Pre-social | Galaxies |
| Symbiotic | Planets |
| Impulsive | Earth system |
| Self-protective | Mutual ecosystems |
| Conformist | Societies; shared labour |
| Conscientious | Groups/families |
| Individualistic | Tribes/Villages |
| Autonomous | Early state/empire |
| Integrated | Nations |
| Interior collective | Exterior collective |

The model:

- Fits together subjective feelings and objective assessments
- Shows the different values of the arts and the sciences
- Shows the stages of development for each activity (more complex towards the outside).

Key characteristics of development within this model:

- Activities are self chosen, cannot be taught
- The reward is greater development or understanding
- Levels reveal themselves when understood – "oh, that's what I was doing"
- Therefore it is risky at all levels
- Healthy development is balanced, emphasis in one area (or a block at one level) will create disharmony, probably leading to a poor social fit, e.g. impulsive, egocentric or ethnocentric behaviour.

Do some of these statements look familiar? I hope so because I believe that Play is how we explore these four quadrants both as children and later in life.

## Play Descriptions and the Wilber Model

To help with understanding this model, I have placed some of the commonly accepted play types[135] within the Wilber Model.

| **Subjective** **Intentional –** **Individual identity** | **Objective** **Behavioural –** **Physical skills** |
|---|---|
| Deep play<br>Symbolic play<br>Creative play | Mastery<br>Rough and tumble<br>Object play<br>Exploratory play<br>Locomotor play |
| Symbolic play<br>Role play<br>Creative play<br>Dramatic play<br>Imaginative play<br>Fantasy play<br>**Cultural –** **Relationships for the child** | Rough and tumble<br>Communication play<br>Social play<br>Socio dramatic play<br><br>**Social frameworks –** **Status and politics** |

We can see that the types of play currently identified fit within the model to show how each separately contributes to healthy development within the individual. It is also possible to state that a 'block' in development may lead to the individual staying at one level, mainly developing only in one quadrant or area, or simply repeating one type of activity over and over.

## Overview – the Play Cycle

I believe that play is the manifestation of a basic drive for us to explore the world around us. My explanation (based on previous work by Gordon Sturrock and Stephen Rennie) is as follows. The full play cycle, as described by psycholudics[136] (the study of the mind at play), is shown in the diagram below.

---

[135] These play descriptions are as categorised by Bob Hughes (1996) in *A playworker's taxonomy of play types*, PLAYLINK, London UK

[136] Gordon Sturrock and Perry Else (1998), *The playground as therapeutic space: playwork as healing* (known as 'The Colorado Paper'), published in *Play in a Changing Society: Research, Design, Application*, IPA/USA Triennial National Conference, Little Rock, USA

134

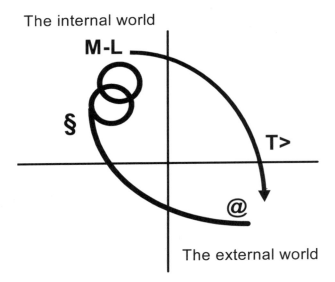

The internal world

M-L

§

T>

@

The external world

The play drive comes from the internal play source (ML) of the child, who issues play cues into the environment. Play cues will decay over time (T>) unless they interact (@) with another person or a stimulus in the environment. This play return is then processed (§) by the child, who may choose to extend the play by issuing another play cue. This is the complete play cycle. The process is described in more detail in the following sections.

## Internal Play Source

In our experience of play, we have seen children move from a game that tests their physical skill, to one that tests their friendships, to one that tests their courage, to one that tests us, the adult representative of society. And this has happened unconsciously, subconsciously and frequently in a far quicker time than it has taken to describe it – the child is playing and there are no limits!

The space where these actions come from is concerned with all aspects of the child's well being; physical, psychological, emotional and societal. This space is in constant flux between each of these states and is concerned with all and none of them, it is beyond them. We describe this place as the *metalude*. This is a technical term meaning 'changing play space' or 'play transformation space', but we feel that it is important to understand this concept to understand all that follows. This space would never be found in the physical brain of the child but we, as playworkers, are aware of its existence and the influence it exerts on children at play. It is the internal space where play is created and processed in the mind of the child.

Children at play are 'alive in the moment', with no concern for the past or future. Playworkers feel these moments through their experiences with children, although the external, physical evidence is slight.

The meeting between the child and the adult in any play setting involves an 'overlapping' of these moments. In some play experiences, the child's and the playworker's individuality merge to form a new, joint identity. This happens when people play together and 'get lost' in their play. Overall, this experience is a valuable and pleasant experience for all involved. However, as playworkers, we need to be aware of the potential abdication of responsibility that may happen if we become more engrossed in the play than in the work responsibility.

## Play Drive

We believe that children are *driven* to play. They will play beyond most physical and psychological boundaries – the need for food, sleep, toilet, rules, prohibitions and fears. The play drive is the term we give to what arises in the 'internal play space' of the child. The drive is the child's urge to experience and test all that is around them. It is a necessary part of existence and the suppression of this drive causes problems for the child either immediately or later in life. Again, this has been experienced many times by playworkers in their daily role.

If the child is confident and finds someone or something stopping their play, they will usually find a way round it. This creative act may bring them into immediate conflict with an authority figure. If the child is insecure, they may blame themselves for the problem, internalise the suppression, and so stop developing an important aspect of their personality. This may not appear again for many years until the child feels confident to face the block, play through it, and consequently feel better.

## Play Frame

There are many descriptions of the importance of the physical environment for 'framing' or holding the child's play. Frequently these descriptions only look at the physical space seen by the worker. However, in any play setting there will be many 'play frames' overlapping simultaneously and playworkers need to be sensitive to these. These frames are not just physical but involve the projected thoughts of the child at play.

In a given play setting, there will be children moving freely about the space, interacting with others, lost in their game. There will also be quiet groups of two or three individuals similarly lost in a private game or drama. There may even be a solitary individual deep in thought to him or herself. This may be the thought of joyful reflection or may be the sorrow of loss or neglect. The physical environment will be the same but the children's experiences will be different for each individual. It is this range of frames of which the worker needs to be aware; some will lead to play, others will not.

These frames can last literally seconds to many weeks. The joy (or trauma) may pass and the action will move on; or the game may be extended through many levels and depths of involvement – such as traditional den building where the play goes through scrounging, building, acting, adaptation, destruction, to name just a few of the play uses. The frame will last a long as it has relevance and meaning for the projected play form of the child.

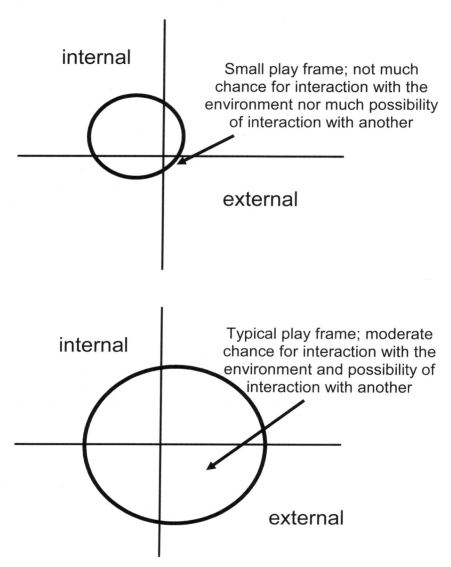

The most important function of the frame is that it provides the context or stage where the play form is made real. In healthy play, the frame is chosen and initiated by the child. It is a holder of meaning for the child and can be used as a reflector for this meaning. The play frame becomes ineffective when it can no longer provide this reflection or return. The play frame can therefore be seen as a child initiated, non-material constraint or boundary that helps define and give meaning to play content.

## Play Cues

When children are playing, they are driven to issue play cues from the play source (the metalude) and to form the play frame. The play cue is the invitation from the child to the surrounding environment to join in play of one sort or another. The play worker, in order to interact with the child, needs to respond to these cues in a variety of ways. Understanding this process largely informs how we then work with the child.

If we recognise that play is a form of consciousness, the play cue is the signal for the world to engage with the child's developing sense of self and reality – 'things as they are'. From the responses generated, the child's sense of self, their personal life-world is developed. Sidoli and Davis say this as follows; 'the quality of [our] life depends on how far we are able to play out and live what is within us.'[137] It is only by recognising this vitally important fact that we can begin to appreciate the effects of intervention and involvement in the play of the child.

The play cue may not always be a positive prompt; it could be an emotional or anxious outburst that is seen as attention seeking. The concerned playworker should be able to read and respond to all manners of cues in a way appropriate to the situation. The playworker should have a range of responses to the play cue if they are to work effectively in the child's play space (this is expanded in the next section). Play cues are issued with the expectation of response or return and when this does not take place frustration occurs; the play cycle can become corrupted. This corruption can be the source of dysfunctional play behaviours.

## Play Return

The response to the play cue is the play return. In play, the response or return may come from the environment. The child issues a playful intent that is 'reflected' by the environment, the child sees or experiences something that completes the play loop and encourages the play to continue.

More frequently, the return will come from another child or a playworker. The play return is the material that the playworker introduces to extend or enhance the children's play – it is the appropriate response to the various themes that the children uncover and express.

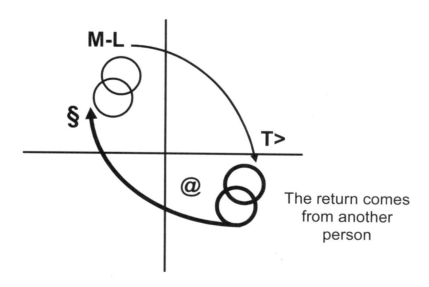

The return comes from another person

[137] Sidoli and Davis (1988), *Jungian Child Psychotherapy*, Karnac Books, London UK

The child could be exploring its first experience of death, say after finding a dead bird under a bush.[138] The worker can react to the child coming to share this with them in one of three basic ways. The first is to express disgust and to tell the child to 'drop that dirty thing'. The second would be to ignore the child and let them explore for themselves. The third way would be to engage with the child and their curiosity and to ask and answer the 'how' and 'why' kind of questions. Only the last example will potentially extend the play; the first will stop it cold, the second adds nothing.

The challenge for us as playworkers is that we need to make these play returns 'moment to moment' as we are interacting with the children. Additionally, as has been said, there may also be several overlapping play frames in the play space and all of these will need separate and individual judgements in order to enhance the play without adulterating or inhibiting it.

## The Response – Loop and Flow

When the child gains a return from the environment, that return is 'processed' back in the internal play space, the 'play transformation space' or metalude. Again the process is far quicker than I am able to describe but goes something like this. The child responds to the cue, finds something in it of interest, decides to engage with that aspect and issues another or related play cue, which then starts the play cycle off again. The process is described as a 'loop and flow' (§) to try to capture the freedom with which the child is able to engage with any aspect of the play return. Children freely playing are capable of changing roles, rules and games within seconds.

These descriptions illustrate the complete cycle of play. Play is not just the behaviour that children exhibit when playing, nor is it solely the physical or social activities seen. Play is a much more subtle and dynamic process that requires sensitive interaction by skilled people. Many of us have known this for many years, yet our practice does not use this experience as its prime 'reason for being.' Instead, we focus on practical play skill acquisition or the safety elements of the physical environment as being more important. The psycholudic approach suggests that we need to refocus our efforts on what happens in the play cycle in order to understand its complete dynamics and the influence on developing children.

---

[138] Thanks to Steve Chown for starting this story

## Practice Applications

### Authenticity

Being honest and open with children is one of the most important things we can do with them. Part of growing up is learning to understand the difference between fantasy and reality. Keeping children cocooned in an unreal world where nothing bad ever happens will disadvantage them as they grow older. This is not a request that all children are introduced to the horrors of the world at the age of three, but it is to ask that when they show they are ready to enquire about such things that we give a mature response. It is when we corrupt their thinking by offering our own prejudices as the 'truth' of a situation that we do the greatest harm. Children need to be offered breadth and depth in the responses from the adults around them if they are to be best able to make sense of their world.

At times this may involve letting them know how upset or angry we are about what they have done; they need to see that we are human too. The child will understand far more if reprimands can be couched in terms of the problem, what was wrong, rather than a lazy, emotional outburst attacking the child as a person – 'Oh Susan, <u>you</u> always get things wrong.' Being able to be honest with ourselves is necessarily part of the need to be honest and authentic with children. This is a difficult task, as it will involve us facing and challenging our own blocks, understanding those – and accordingly ourselves – could be a painful process. This is where the support of an effective play team becomes essential to the play work process.

### Reflection – Before and After Play

For several years, the playwork profession has spoken of the reflective approach to playwork. At its simplest this approach requires a regular review of the work practice to make sure that the planned programme achieved its outputs; in enlightened playworkers this reflection also includes their own behaviours and attitudes. It has become common with the introduction of the National Vocational Qualification to hear of workers reflecting in a systematic way in order to collect evidence towards their portfolio. We are suggesting a much more dynamic and integrated approach. Reflection is essential to understanding why we react to situations in certain ways. This approach recognises that the choices we make are influenced by the beliefs and attitudes we hold as well as our own emotional security (or lack of it).

The playwork team has a responsibility to help each other in this reflective task both before and after the playwork session. Again, this is something that playworkers have always done intuitively; but we are talking here about more than the pre-work coffee or post-work drink. Before work, the job is to help each other prepare for the work to come by considering what may arise in the coming session or programme. By examining how we will react to certain themes or material, we are better prepared to be a resource to the children. This preparation may include for example, consideration of the ecological impact of the activity, or how certain roles in a game carry positive or negative values. How would we help the children understand these issues; would we lecture, discuss or let the child find out for themselves? A little forethought would help supply the answers to these questions.

It may also arise that the playwork session will produce themes and material that could not be predicted. Playworkers will then need to form quick judgements about what to do. The post-session, team reflection will help with understanding how the worker's judgement or intervention was useful. This reflection should allow staff to examine their own particular responses to the play themes, ideas and symbolism that developed in the play work session. Our own perceptions will be filtered through our own particular heritage or the knowledge and events we have experienced to date. Playwork, in 1999, necessarily involves children from a wide variety of cultures and backgrounds, who may have different cultural legacies to our own. While we have now legislated for workers to accept and work with these differences, our work can be so much more than just recognition of difference. Children need workers who are culturally competent themselves, workers able to recognise the elements of a strong culture in order to support it or debate with it.

## Containment

The support that workers can give to children in play should include the ability to hold or 'contain' the play. Containment is not intended in a pejorative sense here; it is about supporting a child through their initial tentative play cues, giving back a return to help the play on its way, being 'co-present' as the child extends their boundaries. We need to remember that very little of the developed environment is 'virgin territory' for children. There is not much left that has not been 'concretised', controlled, adapted or 'made safe'. Some children need to learn how to learn skills in what is generally a hostile environment for them. The playworker gives a gentle help to the child at a critical stage, encouraging them to develop a wider play frame, one that includes as many cultural possibilities as it will hold.

Containment should also be about helping children who may be at risk of harming themselves or others. Enthusiastic children can easily extend their frame to include the whole of the environment around them; this may bring them into conflict with other users of that environment. Playworkers will need to bring the play back to a safe or tolerable level. This will necessarily involve some diminution of the play, but a sensitive playworker will be attuned to this. They will be aware of the potential for adulteration of the play cycle and will strive to satisfy the child's play drive in a culturally appropriate way. The use of rituals and rites is a valuable aid in containing play in a healthy way for children.

## Rites and Rituals

Playwork already has many rituals that we celebrate throughout the day, the week and the year. The annual rituals are easy to spot, and we may be aware of the daily and weekly rituals, which will be different on each play site. Some rituals will be set by the workers, some by the children. Workers' rituals usually include a winding down activity in the last half-hour of the playwork session, or a fire or den building session at the weekend. Children will have their own initiations into various games, ways of choosing team players or challenges to prove the maturity of individuals.

Workers can extend these rituals to include positive ways of bringing games to a close, or to provide a containing context for the play until the child or children are next on the site; they provide a finalisation or completion to the play that will help the child leave the game and their role in a healthy way. Examples of this would be say putting a 'chapter ending' into a story, or agreeing that the next complete stage of the game will end it for today ('first one to score a goal').

More valuable still would be when workers help with the realisation or transcendent aspects of play and life. Workers can show children that they have 'moved on' by the use of rituals. We can help children gain in confidence when they carry out exceptional acts. For some children it may be their first appearance on stage, for others their first camp away from home, or simply the first time they were able to use a piece of equipment unaided. Recognising these acts in a formal way, rather than simply with a pat on the back, will help the child see the significance of the act and learn more from it.

I have also known some playgrounds hold a 'leaving ceremony' for young people who have outgrown the use of the playground but have not yet detached emotionally from it. The ceremony helps them make the change in a positive way, rather than feel they have been pushed out. If the ceremony is planned with the young people, they will get used to the idea of separation and be more ready for it when it happens.

## Support and Counselling

It may be that a worker tries to push a child out of the play site because in their opinion the child 'does not fit'. This would be adulteration and must be challenged by other workers. The best way to deal with this would be through the reflective session before or after the play session. We need to recognise that the worker may be playing out a personal fantasy and will need release from that fantasy if they are to move on themselves.

Often simply recognising the behaviour may be enough to help them make the change, though we should be aware that at times more focused counselling might be appropriate. I am not advocating that playworkers take on this role, but being attuned to it, they can help colleagues seek out such help. Additionally, formal appraisal sessions instigated by the management team will help with the exposure or realisation of such needs. Moreover, blunt though it sounds, workers unable to change should be removed from the environment – though this is often difficult to achieve in practice.

## Factors of a Play Enabling Environment

So far, I have focused on the efforts of the play team, but just as valuable, perhaps even more valuable, is the quality of the environment for play. As is now widely recognised, the modern environment is not play friendly. If we accept that the child can gain a play return from a play-enabling environment, we are depriving them of their right to play in much of the modern environment. More frightening still, is that in the main, the defined playgrounds for children are now so designed that any sense of playfulness is completely absent – 'we are seeing the gradual diminishing of the child's right to reverie, imagination and fantasy.' [139] As a society, we tend to be obsessed with the safety of play equipment, the number of swings, their seat design and their colour. We should instead be concentrating on the quality of the environment so that it provides stimulus, fun, release, and life enhancing and therapeutic aspects.

Such an environment has been frequently described by Bob Hughes and others but to repeat it would include: the natural elements, fabricated and natural materials, challenge, movement; stimulus for the senses, opportunities for playing with identity, for social interactions, change, and overall be an interesting and varied physical environment. This range and variety of elements gives children opportunities to develop in a range of ways across all quadrants of the model.

## Training Implications – Choice not a 'Force Fed' Approach

We have also been saying for many years that provision should also be child directed, child influenced, free to come and go, supported by sensitive adults. If this long cherished statement about play is not to be lost in the rush to turn us all into care workers or education workers, we need to say very clearly that growth, learning and ultimately, self healing, does not come through being 'force-fed' the message. I know I'm repeating what will be obvious to most playworkers but this message needs saying loud and long; education is not the way to create healthy, balanced individuals; to mis-quote the old saw, 'You can take a child to school, but you cannot make them think'.

## Natural Playworkers and Others

The person whom I call the 'natural playworker' has always understood this. The natural playworker is the balanced individual who knows how and when to intervene in the play of the child and when to leave well alone. They will have a repertoire of responses to the child when necessary that will include the ability to be controlling without being

---

[139] Gordon Sturrock (2002), *North of the Future – Reverie, Imagination and Fantasy as a Ludic Ecology*, Ludemos Associates, London

aggressive, and encourage free play without being weak or passive. To offer a quality play provision, we need to be sure that all workers have these skills.

What concerns me about the majority of our current play training is that it does not cover all the aspects of play, it does not 'see the whole of the picture.'

## Playwork Content

To come back to the point, does play training help us to know what it is that play is? Learning all the games in the world will not facilitate play if the worker leading those games is not in tune with the play cues that the children will be issuing. They will not be aiding play if they have a limited range of responses to children that offers no growth or stimulus to the cue of the child. Training offers tools that workers can use, but frequently it is up to the worker to interpret when the tool is appropriate. We support this interpretation by offering experiential learning, but again the logic is that understanding what play is, is learned by osmosis, from other, successful playworkers.

The psycholudic model is intended to be a way of making the structures of play more explicit and therefore more easily understood. Overall, we are aiming to create workers who are balanced and healthy individuals, able to make sound, culturally aware decisions.

We are not intending to produce workers who are merely mechanistic, who are able to show their competence across a range of quantifiable but developmentally dry topics. While the development of the NVQs have helped many individuals who are working in play gain some recognition and confidence from their long held experiences, like some training, they have not helped in the validation and description of what it is that play is. To return again to my opening story seeing the whole picture, play is not just about, say, behavioural development. True play is also about personal expression, skill rehearsal and cultural understanding. True play work should encompass all these aspects and should encourage operation across many developmental levels. The currently available NVQs need extending to recognise these points.

How practical is all this? To take just a few of the ideas I can give an example from a student placement who I have recently been supervising. This first year student on the BA (Hons) playwork course at Leeds wanted to observe the operation of play cues. We put together the following sheet as a tool for aiding that observation.

The student, Gill Ward, reported no difficulty at all in spotting play cues, play returns and play frames. In fact her observations showed that the speed of the interchange, the depth of responses, and the integration of various ideas within the play were all far greater than she had imagined. As a worker she felt that being able to respond to cues would not be problematic, and has already started integrating these concepts in her day-to-day work.

## Play – Observation Checklist

Date  Venue

Child  Age  Gender  Other

Time observation started  Time observation ended

### Play Cue

| **Spoken** | direct | indirect | third party | |
|---|---|---|---|---|
| Non spoken | indirect invitation | eye contact | touch | object |
| Emotion displayed | fun | non aggressive | aggressive | |

Duration before response (time)  Repetition before response
(frequency)

Description of cue:

### Play Return From

| Self generated/ environment | Another child | Adult | Worker |
|---|---|---|---|
| | | | |

Description of return:

Comment: (positive, negative, enhancements, adulteration)

### Play Frame

Frame adopted by child

Frame clearly established by child

Frame not visible to observer

### Use of play frame:

By child  By others


### Summary

There are many exciting developments in the world of playwork at the moment and a lot of good work has been done in recent years to raise the status of play and play work. In doing so we should not be afraid to state in forceful terms what many of us have felt for years, that play is fundamental to the development of children. Play is more than a rehearsal for adulthood, more than behavioural development, more than personal expression. It is a whole that is more than the sum of its parts, and – fundamentally – it is to do with the child's developmental well-being in the widest possible sense.

If we can carry that thought with us throughout our work, we will better be able to serve children and playwork, our profession.


**Perry Else**
June 1999

Therapeutic Playwork Reader one 1995-2000

# A New Way of Seeing

Perry Else

## Welcome

Most people like sunsets. Show a full red sunset to any group of people of whatever background, age or education and most of them will feel touched. Ask them what the sunset means to them and you would probably get a range of replies that covered the following:

- The colour of the sunset; the red sun descending and flushing the sky with golden pink
- The spectacle of the event, the sense of awe and majesty
- The peace at the end of the day, with the rest of night to come
- The promise of the new day in the morning, the certainty that the sun will rise again.

Can the sunset be described using only one of these replies? Would that reply serve for everyone who was seeing the event? Would the importance and significance be captured?

Looking at play holds similar questions for me.

## A True Theory of Play?

Reviewing some of the commonly accepted theories of play, I came across the following main categories:

- The physiological and biological approaches – children play to develop their bodies and physical skills
- The psychological approach – play as a way of dealing with trauma, play as emotion
- The cognitive/developmental approach – play as intellectual development
- The socio-cultural approach – skills and role practice for later life.

All of these theories can find evidence to prove their validity; all of them are true from a given point of view. But how can all of these theories claim be representative of the phenomenon that is play? Which one was the true theory?

In this presentation I shall introduce you to a model that gives an integrated view of personal development, I shall describe the characteristics of that model and how I feel they fit within a playwork context. Then I shall briefly explain a way of understanding play that can maximise on this approach, commenting on some of the implications within society and the playwork field as I do.

**Seeing the Whole Picture – The Wilber 'All Quadrant' Model**

This model first proposed by Ken Wilber[140] shows how human development occurs in four key quadrants that represent the interior and exterior worlds and the individual and collective perspectives. Healthy development occurs when growth or development occurs or is encouraged in all four quadrants.

| ARTS<br>**Interior individual** | SCIENCES<br>**Exterior individual** |
|---|---|
| Concepts | Complex brain |
| Symbols | Reptilian brain system |
| Emotion | Neural cord |
| Impulse | Neuronal organisms |
| Perception | Single celled animals |
| Sensation | Molecules |
| Irritability | Atoms |
| Pre-social | Galaxies |
| Symbiotic | Planets |
| Impulsive | Earth system |
| Self-protective | Mutual ecosystems |
| Conformist | Societies; shared labour |
| Conscientious | Groups/families |
| Individualistic | Tribes/Villages |
| Autonomous | Early state/empire |
| Integrated | Nations |
| **Interior collective** | **Exterior collective** |

The model:

- Fits together subjective feelings and objective assessments
- Shows the different value of the arts and the sciences
- Shows the stage of development for each activity (more complex towards the outside).

The key characteristics of development within this model are:

- Activities are self chosen, cannot be taught
- The reward is greater development or understanding
- Levels reveal themselves when understood – 'oh, that's what I was doing'.
- Therefore it is risky at all levels

---

[140] Ken Wilber (1998), *The Marriage of Sense and Soul*, Random House, New York USA

- Healthy development is balanced; emphasis in one area (or a block at one level) will create disharmony, probably leading to a poor social fit, e.g. impulsive, egocentric or ethnocentric behaviour.

Do some of these statements look familiar? I hope so, because I believe that Play is how we explore these four quadrants both as children and later in life.

## Play Descriptions and the Wilber Model

To help with understanding this model, I have placed some of the commonly accepted play types[141] within the Wilber Model.

| **Subjective**<br>**Intentional –**<br>**Individual identity** | **Objective**<br>**Behavioural –**<br>**Physical skills** |
|---|---|
| Deep play<br>Symbolic play<br>Creative play | Mastery<br>Rough and tumble<br>Object play<br>Exploratory play<br>Locomotor play |
| Symbolic play<br>Role play<br>Creative play<br>Dramatic play<br>Imaginative play<br>Fantasy play<br>**Cultural –**<br>**Relationships for the child** | Rough and tumble<br>Communication play<br>Social play<br>Socio dramatic play<br><br>**Social frameworks –**<br>**Status and politics** |

We can see that the types of play currently identified fit within the model to show how each separately contributes to healthy development within the individual. It is also possible to state that a 'block' in development may lead to the individual staying at one level, mainly developing only in one quadrant or area, or simply repeating one type of activity over and over.

## Overview – the Play Cycle

I believe that play is the manifestation of a basic drive for us to explore the world around us. My explanation (based on previous work by Gordon Sturrock and Stephen Rennie) is as follows. The full play cycle,

---

[141] These play descriptions are as categorised by Bob Hughes (1996), in *A Playworker's Taxonomy of Play Types*, PLAYLINK, London UK

as described by psycholudics[142] (the study of the mind at play), is shown in the diagram below.

The internal world

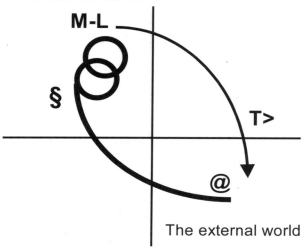

The external world

The play drive comes from the internal play source, the metalude (ML) of the child, who issues play cues into the environment. Play cues will decay over time (T>) unless they interact (@) with another person or a stimulus in the environment. This play return is then processed (§) by the child, who may choose to extend the play by issuing another play cue. This is the complete play cycle. This play cycle will occur within a play frame, a flexible, non-material boundary initiated by the child in the internal world that helps define and give meaning to the play in the external world.

Play is the process by which we test out our understanding of the development field we are currently in. It is the way we 'play' with concepts and skills that we do not yet understand. It is also what we do when we want to have fun.

Through the Wilber model, we can see that play is how we find out about our own internal world (ourselves), the subjective relationships we have with others (our community and culture), and the wider world (the objective world we share with others).

We can also use the model to describe how children (and people) can operate at different stages in their development. While simple operation at a given level may be healthy for the person's age and ability, problems can occur where development is blocked, the person is afraid, or does not have the confidence to move on.

There is also the problem of people who only operate mainly in one quadrant (or type of development), or who are only offered experiences

---

[142] G Sturrock and P Else (1998), *The playground as therapeutic space: playwork as healing* (known as 'The Colorado Paper'), published in *Play in a Changing Society: Research, Design, Application*, The IPA/USA Triennial National Conference, Little Rock, USA

from that area. Where playworkers restrict or dominate the play cues of children, we rightly give the term 'adulteration' to the action – where the adult perspective is forced onto children in an attempt to educate them or for their 'safety'. Examples of all these problems are expanded in the next section.

## How Problems can Manifest in Play

In recent times, we have tended to judge people by either their subjective abilities (for example as artists) or their objective thinking (as scientists). While these two definitions are the two main halves of the four quadrants, it is possible to see other behaviour traits through using the model.

## The Individual/Intentional Quadrant

When children do not develop beyond the impulse and emotional stages in the development of their own internal state, they may tend to find simple bodily sensation seeking as the only goal in life. They would be unable to understand the world through complicated symbols and would find conceptual thinking very difficult. The world for them would exist through the feelings in their body.

A person who operates mainly in this quadrant would have poorly developed social skills, be unable to relate to others and would have a weak physical awareness.

## The Collective/Cultural Quadrant

In this quadrant, we find the range of levels from self protective ego based through to individualistic or existentialist behaviour. All of these can produce problems, as they would affect the ability of the individual to interact with others to form a culture. Self-protective people would find it difficult to trust others and would tend to alienate themselves from the dominant culture. When existentialist behaviour becomes nihilistic, it can be dangerous for either the individual or those around them.

Someone who operates mainly in this quadrant would only be able to experience the world through other people, they would have a poorly developed sense of their own abilities.

## The External/Behavioural Quadrant

While the descriptions given in this area relate to the highest stages of physical development, that is the complex brain, it should be remembered that the ability to manipulate and use our bodies goes along with that complex development. Problems in this area may be created by a poor sense of the external world, our own bodies and the abilities they are capable of. I would dare to say that our (in the UK) current obsession with the physical safety of play areas comes from the collective lack of development in this area by the current dominant generation.

A person who only develops in this quadrant would tend to have a good sense of their physical abilities but have a weak imagination, and lack cultural values.

## The Social/Collective Quadrant

This quadrant is where societal frameworks are developed through family groups, then tribes, states and then nations. When the child stays at the tribal or early state in social development, the behaviour can be exhibited as parochialism or as a fear of others as xenophobia or racism. As children develop, they would get a sense of group dynamics or interplay between individuals and would be able to test this out through their social play, seeing who was 'leader' etc. I also feel that an overemphasis on the collective social world leads to play provision that is geared mainly for the benefit of society and not the individual, hence we develop child care provision that meets the needs of adults and may or may not serve the needs of children. My plea through all this would be that we aim for a balanced provision that meets all needs of the individual, which would necessarily develop as they take their place in society.

While I have tried to give simple descriptions of types of behaviour and attitudes from the four quadrants, it may also be apparent that combinations of levels of development (or lack of it) can lead to other characteristics. For example, a child who is obsessed with self-protection and is operating at the group or tribal level is likely to feel violent towards the dominant social group, or the group that they see as having more power than them. They would tend to associate solely with their own group and see that group as their only purpose in life.

We can also see how people with disabilities may be penalised in different ways. There is first the nature of their disability that may affect their ability to grow. For instance, a physical disability may restrict ability in a given area. However, the more damaging aspect would be the perception of others, especially carers who may assume that a weakness in one area would lead to weakness in all. The person may then be given restricted opportunities that further prevent a compensating development in the other quadrants. Essential to understanding this is that while a balanced approach may be the optimum objective, it is not essential or even necessary to be good in one area in order to excel at the highest level in another. The most powerful example of that is Professor Stephen Hawking, the most eminent physicist of his generation yet unable to speak or move about by his own means.

There is also the phenomenon of 'dysplay', where the child issues play cues in a desperate attempt to interact with others or to learn from the environment around them. Children unable to process a play return from another or unable to find stimulus of their own will become dysfunctional and probably antisocial; this may be the syndrome currently described as attention deficit disorder. These children would remain stuck at their current level of development with little opportunity to change or improve. Over time, it is likely that the behaviour would become automatic and so the only way that the child operates. We would argue that interaction with a skilled playworker to expand and help with understanding the issued cues of the child will be more therapeutic in the long term than the current practice of sedation.

## A Practical Summary

While this may seem over complex and beyond the practical range of people working daily in play, I believe the core concepts are simple and can form the core of our practice.

- Play is the way we test and develop our understanding of both the subjective, internal world and the objective, physical world. It is how we understand ourselves and those around us.

- Play provision should facilitate and encourage development of the individual's mind and body, their culture and their understanding of power relationships, equality and politics.

- The play cycle describes the process of play as it unfolds. Workers who recognise and understand play cues and play frames and who offer appropriate play returns will encourage healthy play development. These concepts can be communicated simply and in a practical way for workers just starting out in their play work careers. Helping with this understanding should be the duty of all managers of provision and playwork trainers.

More work needs to be done to test and expand on these concepts; however, there is evidence to show that the model can be used in this simple way. While the use of the four-quadrant model is currently limited, there are several projects in the UK where workers are using psycholudics on a daily basis across a range of disciplines. The early indications are that workers welcome the fundamental concepts, and have already begun to use the terms as a means of communicating with their colleagues. They have already been used by several training publications to communicate the understanding of what is at the heart of the play process, and are being used in national pilots looking at playwork quality and standard setting.

## Conclusions

In this presentation, I have tried to stress the fundamental importance of play to the healthy, balanced development of human beings. The drive to play is the tool the human condition has created as way of testing and developing ourselves, our society and the environment through which we move.

Understanding this importance, we should challenge those who 'misuse' play to control or repress children, whether consciously or unknowingly. Play is much more than a simple response to a controlled stimulus presented by adults; children do not just play in the allotted playgrounds.

We need to ensure that our own practice is balanced in terms of helping children develop their minds, their bodies, their emotions and their understanding of the objective world, both in terms of its dynamics and the politics of relationships. To do this we need to help children understand and use the concept of power.

Further, we need to be sure that our play workers are conscious in how they work with and relate to children. This will require workers who are self-confident and have a high regard for both themselves and others, who are mature in their understanding of all quadrants so that they can encourage and support development in others.

Stimulating environments will help with encouraging children to experience on their own and with others. An environment with a variety of stimuli will aid growth in the creative, social, cultural and physical spheres of development.

Workers will need to reflect and evaluate their practice on a daily basis. This reflection should encompass the widest range of responses to the events on site. It should not just focus on the management aspects of the provision but also on the quality of the play experiences facilitated. This reflection should ideally be team based with workers helping each other to develop their own understanding and so themselves alongside the provision.

Overall, I am aiming to offer a new way of seeing the wonderful phenomenon that is play. A way of seeing that captures the values and approaches that we have identified intuitively through our practice and that now have a common language to speak of their importance.

**Perry Else**
June 1999

# A Wonder Full Profession

Perry Else

*'Everyone here has looked at a newborn baby and has been filled with wonder. Each time I see a newly born child, I am filled with hope and a sense of awe. Because what I am witnessing, is the greatest act of creation in the history of the universe.*

*No other event, neither the birth of a star nor the collision of planets is as significant as that child. The throwing up of mountain ranges by the clash of moving continents is insignificant when measured against the significance of one human being.*

*Mountains, planets, stars and great oceans are moved by forces outside themselves. That child, and every person here and every person born into the world has the gift of life, which places the power within themselves.*

*No matter how high the mountains, with all their grandeur, get their heads into the heavens, they are unable to ask one simple question. The Niagara Falls with all their tremendous power will never know the fragrance of a rose and a volcanic eruption capable of blocking out the sun will never experience an act of love.'* [143]

I hope that these words from Paddy Doherty have moved you, as they moved me. What an awesome thought – each and every child born into this world is that important; they are more significant and more valuable than the greatest forces in nature. Perhaps even more awesome (or is it frightening) is that each of us as playworkers has taken on a responsibility to encourage and support that growth.

Do we feel that responsibility in our day to day work? Do we encourage that potential through our work? Are we recognised by the wider community as a profession that has a fundamental role in such a development? The first two questions I'll leave for you to think over while we work through today; the last I'll aim to expand on in the next few minutes.

The question really has two parts; is play recognised as important and are playworkers seen as important in facilitating play? I think that Play *is* and *isn't* recognised. It is recognised because 'everyone' knows that children need to play; most parents and even most adults will recognise that children learn something through play, or will see that children enjoy play and on that basis they see it as a good thing.

But that recognition also leads to the devaluation of play. As to what play really is, most people will struggle to find words to describe it. They see it as a natural part of growing up, and as such, it loses its importance. If it is 'natural' then it will happen anyway and why should we spend money on it?

---

[143] Paddy Doherty (19 September 1997), from *Here To Stay*, the proceedings of the Conference organised by the Development Trusts Association, London

There is currently a national programme looking at the outcomes from playwork and part of that work will to try to show the benefits of playwork and why money should be set aside by government for its provision. My contribution to that debate has been to say that play covers four aspects of human development, and so the outcomes from playwork should be significant in those four areas.

The advantage we human beings have over stars, planets and mountains is that we have an interior as well as an exterior world; we are able to think and communicate, as well as exist and fit into the material world. A model of human development that I have developed, based on a model from Ken Wilber,[144] shows how these aspects of our world can be described as intentional, cultural, behavioural and social. That is, what we know of ourselves as individuals, how we relate to those around us, how we operate in the world, the physical skills we develop, and our place in the social structure. I believe that play is the way we experiment and learn about these four fundamental aspects of ourselves.

### The child's world – a fuller picture[145]

| **Subjective**<br>**Intentional –**<br>**Individual identity** | **Objective**<br>**Behavioural –**<br>**Physical skills** |
|---|---|
| Deep play<br>Symbolic play<br>Creative play | Mastery<br>Rough and tumble<br>Object play<br>Exploratory play<br>Locomotor play |
| Symbolic play<br>Role play<br>Creative play<br>Dramatic play<br>Imaginative play<br>Fantasy play<br>**Cultural –**<br>**Relationships for the child** | Rough and tumble<br>Communication play<br>Social play<br>Socio dramatic play<br><br>**Social frameworks –**<br>**Status and politics** |

Play is what we as human beings do instinctively to explore these four areas of our complete world. Through play we learn to:

1. recognise new skills and behaviours,
2. practise them till competent and then
3. integrate them into our 'portfolio' of skills and behaviours, which then shape who and what we are.

---

[144] Ken Wilber (1996), *A Brief History of Everything*, Gill & Macmillan Ltd, Dublin

[145] These play descriptions are as categorised by Bob Hughes (1996), in *A Playworker's Taxonomy of Play Types*, PLAYLINK, London UK

There are two important concepts in this. Firstly, that the act of playing is the action that takes us to the next level in our development. We do this freely, for its own sake and not without a little fear, because of the risk of the unknown, that we might fail or get hurt. Early in our development, we are learning the fundamentals to do with walking and running, later on to do with thoughts and feelings and finally with a sense of self and connectedness with others.

Secondly, that healthy development comes from a balance of the four aspects. To simplify, living only in the internal world would cut us off from other people, or an overemphasis on the physical may lead to a lack of sensitivity and empathy with others.

## Play Provision – a Fuller Picture

Now at this point I would like to return to the second part of the question that I set myself – the importance of play provision, and at the same time I'll address some of the new developments taking place in playwork.

Looking through the September 1999 edition of the NPFA's PlayToday magazine, I came upon the following current topics in playwork. With the exception of research into play/playwork and the latest theories of play, I think these topics cover the main issues current in playwork. I've also fitted these issues into the four-quadrant framework.

As you can see, by far the majority of topics fall into the objective, external, adult part of playwork. Very little is directed towards the qualitative, subjective half of the model. This highlights for me the dilemma of play/playwork and its relationship with the wider world. Play is an internal activity, a drive that is best directed from within, either consciously or unconsciously by the playing child. Playwork is the process we use to try to help children develop or to compensate them for the inadequacies and lack of freedom in today's environment.

The internal world of play, its intent and its impact on culture are the parts seen as 'natural' by adults. The external world is the part that can be controlled and influenced by others; and which is increasingly getting the majority of the attention.

Playworkers have felt this emphasis on the structures of playwork to be too strong. At least of equal value we feel is the attention given to the understanding of what is happening in the other half of the process, the internal subjective half. If we as practitioners are not aware of what we are doing there, at best we will be contributing nothing to the child's play, at worst we may be intervening in the natural play process in negative and unhelpful ways.

| Subjective<br>Intentional –<br>Play for the Child | Objective<br>Behavioural –<br>The physical provision |
|---|---|
| Music \Dance | Unsuitable people<br>Training guides<br>Play days<br>Playwork outcomes<br>Environments<br>Homezones |
| Experiences of a Down's syndrome child | NSPCC concerns about safety in play<br>Children's rights and participation<br>A Healthy Nation<br>More legislation<br>Legalities of provision<br>Changes in funding for playwork<br>The national training framework<br>The Education Agenda and Curriculum<br>Play care and the out of school provision |
| Cultural –<br>Relationships for the child | Social frameworks –<br>Law and policy |

We have part of the answer; we place great emphasis on the values of play. The key values being variety, fairness, balance and choice. By providing playwork that incorporates these values, we will be at least ensuring that children's provision does not lose out.

So answering the question I set myself again; the wider community values only part of what is important in playwork. By their omission, they could negatively impact on the play process in children. Part of our work should be about helping people see the beauty and creativity in each and every child, and to remind <u>ourselves</u> of that beauty from time to time.

As play providers, we need to become more confident about saying clearly what the whole play process is, how important it is, the role play workers have in encouraging and developing healthy play, and of course, in a safer, legislated environment as required by our social framework.

Today is part of our personal development in taking playwork forward – I hope everyone here has a wonderful day and takes away some hope and perhaps a little awe at the wonder of the work we are trying to do.

**Perry Else**
October 1999

# Also by the same authors

**THE PLAY CYCLE - AN INTRODUCTION TO PSYCHOLUDICS**
**Perry Else and Gordon Sturrock**

❖ Can you spot a play cue?
❖ Do you know whether you've ever interrupted children's play flow or not?
❖ Does annihilation worry you - and should it?!

Presented as a series of short illustrated magazine articles, this CD-ROM provides essential and accessible underpinning knowledge (particularly for those undertaking Level 3 in Playwork) and those that support them. The Play Cycle will also be of interest to anybody who wants to be able to describe the importance of play in their professional roles.

Available from Common Threads Publications Ltd:

Wessex House
Upper Market Street
Eastleigh
Hampshire
SO50 9FD

T: 07000 785215
F: 07000 780625
E: info@commonthreads.org.uk

All our publications are available to order online:

# www.commonthreads.org.uk